THE ART OF MIXING KOJI COCKTAILS

THE ART OF MIXING KOJI COCKTAILS

A practical guide to the world of Koji with a focus on Japanese Sake and Shochu, and their uses in mixed drinks.

By Samuel Boulton

Foreword by
Klára Kopčiková

Kokushu Creative books may be purchased for educational, business or sales promotional use. For more information, please write to Samuel Boulton, sam@kokushu.info

First Edition
Edited By: Carly Dodd
Illustrations By: Alana Patchett
Calligraphy By: Koharu Ono

ISBN: 978-1-3999-1525-0

Printed in the United Kingdom

This book is dedicated to
Klára Kopčiková, Sophia Noke and Dina Gestoso-Mattar.
Three people who made all this possible.

ACKNOWLEDGEMENTS

I owe a multitude of thanks to those who played a role in bringing this book about koji, sake and shochu to life. I had wanted to write this book for some time, but when life presented me with some of the hardest days I'll ever go through, it didn't feel realistic. Remarkably, this book became an integral part of my healing.

First and foremost, I owe immeasurable gratitude to Klára Kopčiková, who stood by me unwaveringly during the most challenging days of my life. Klára has been an indispensable companion on this voyage into the world of sake and shochu, consistently encouraging my quest for knowledge. Klára and I have shared experiences in Japan, at breweries, exploring, eating, and drinking. All of which enriched this project beyond measure. Of course, Klára went above and beyond, sharing her expertise in drink making for this book, even when she didn't have the time.

Sophia Noke, who sacrificed her precious personal time on multiple occasions so I could delve deeper into this topic, also served as an invaluable sounding board throughout my learning process.

Dina Gestoso-Mattar, a steadfast presence in my life, listened attentively and provided invaluable insights, enabling me to effectively convey these words to you.

I am also deeply grateful to bartenders from around the world who contributed their recipes to this project. Your creativity and passion have added a unique and vibrant dimension to its pages.

To all the dedicated sake and shochu enthusiasts, teachers, and nerds across the globe who patiently fielded my questions, no matter how trivial they may have seemed, I offer my sincere thanks. Notable mentions include Erika Haigh, Honami Matsumoto, Michael Tremblay, John Gauntner, Oliver Hilton-Johnson, Sachiko Koyama, and Marie Cheong-Thong.

I extend my heartfelt appreciation to the remarkable team at Japan Distilled, Christopher Pellegrini and Stephen Lyman, whose words and books have expanded my understanding far beyond my initial expectations. Christopher Pellegrini, in particular, provided assistance with the templates in this book, as well as introductions and recommendations to numerous Awamori and Shochu producers.

A special thanks to Stephen Lyman and Matt Alt, whose research on Jokichi Takamine and Koji Whisky made the Koji Whisky section of this book possible.

To Arline Lyons, for her help with some translation work, it would have been a mess without you!

Lastly, I would like to express my gratitude to the customers, friends, and patrons of my bars and events who have made all this possible. Without your support, I wouldn't have pushed myself to learn this much. While it might not seem like much, you played a pivotal role in deepening my comprehension of sake and shochu.
Thank you all, Sam.

CONTENTS

QUOTES

"Thousands of years have gone by since the original invention of Sake. Hundreds of years since TRUE sake and Shochu a bit later. Surely this is proof that these elixirs have put their stamp in our universe..... and they just get better day by day. What else I one say?....."
Marie Cheong-Thong - Chair of The British Sake Association

"In the end, my sake journey has been about people; the lifelong relationships I have formed along the way. Of course, at the heart of it are the brewers: to see first-hand how much passion and craftsmanship goes into making this remarkable drink is truly inspiring."
Erika Haigh - Founder of Kamosu

"Historic Japanese alcoholic drinks all have one thing in common: the power of Koji. Sake, Shochu & Awamori all make use of this wondrous fungus (Japan's national fungus, no less) resulting in a kaleidoscope of flavours, textures and styles that offer some unique mixing and pairing options. Working with these liquids for many years has deepened my appreciation of this wonder-ingredient and the exciting options it provides for sommeliers, mixologists, bartenders, and amateur enthusiasts alike."
Oliver Hilton-Johnson - Director of Tengu Sake

"During my first visit to Japan, I had the opportunity to explore the Akashi-Tai brewery, it was there that I fall in love with Sake and eventually Shochu. I don't view this book as the final destination on my journey; instead, it has inspired me to continue learning, gaining a deeper understanding, and sharing my findings with all of you."
Samuel Boulton - Author

FOREWORD

I want to introduce you to a good friend of mine, Samuel Boulton. I've known Sam for years, and he has a real love for everything related to drinks. His journey through the world of cocktails and his deep dive into Japanese Koji cocktails have been inspiring to watch. I'm excited to share with you his latest work, "The Art of Mixing Koji Cocktails."

Sam's story in the world of cocktails is nothing short of eventful. He's owned bars that have won multiple awards, and he's become a real expert in Japanese drinks, especially sake and shochu. His dedication to understanding these unique drinks and his recent achievements, like becoming a Certified Sake Professional, Sake Scholar, and Shochu Advisor, show just how passionate he is about what he does.

"The Art of Mixing Koji Cocktails" is Sam's way of sharing what he's learned with you. This book isn't just a guide; it's a mix of solid facts about Japanese drinks, known as "kokushu," and modern cocktail-making. Sam's book takes you on a journey through the rich history and culture of kokushu, helping you understand sake, shochu, and awamori, and how these fantastic liquids can make your cocktails unforgettable. Sam's writing is easy to understand, even if you're new to this topic. He's taken the time to make sure anyone, whether you're a beginner or a pro, can enjoy and learn from this book. You won't just learn; you'll have fun exploring the mix of Eastern and Western traditions.

This book is for anyone who wants to learn more, whether you're a bartender looking to try new things or someone who simply loves discovering new flavours. Sam provides tons of recipes (from bartenders around the world) and expert tips, so you can start creating your own cocktails with all kinds of kokushu. It doesn't matter if you're in a bar or at home; most recipes can be easily replicated with common kitchen equipment, are easy to understand, and detailed enough so everyone can have a try!

This is a book that's real, written by someone who's been where he's writing about. Sam literally finished this book while on a journey around Japan, which he spent learning more about sake and shochu from the closest possible proximity. I've had the pleasure of working and learning with Sam for years, and I can tell you that this book is a treasure trove of knowledge, experience, and fun.

As a bartender with my own background in sake and shochu, I can confirm that "The Art of Mixing Koji Cocktails" is a valuable resource. It's not just a book; it's a journey into the world of koji cocktails, guided by an expert on Japanese Sake and Shochu, and that's hard to find. Sam's book is a work of love, and I'm deeply impressed by the expertise he's poured into every page. This foreword only scratches the surface of what you'll find inside. Dive in and start your own adventure into the world of Koji cocktails. I'm sure you'll love it!

Well done, Sam. Have fun friends!
Kanpai, enit?

Klára Kopčiková

CHAPTER ONE
INTRODUCTION

This book began as a beginner's guide to sake. However, after months of fact-checking, pushing the boundaries of my knowledge, and gathering feedback from people worldwide, it evolved into something much more complex. It's no longer a beginner's guide; in fact, it delves deeply into various topics. I found my focus on Koji, a fascinating subject, and then branched out to explore my passions for Sake, Shochu, and Awamori. Within these pages, we will embark on a wide learning journey, delving into the history and modern applications of three ingredients: Koji, Sake, and Shochu. This book is an invitation to explore how these elements seamlessly integrate into contemporary mixology in the world of Japanese alcohol.

Central to this exploration is koji, an enigmatic fermenting agent revered in Japan's brewing history for centuries. This unassuming mould possesses the extraordinary ability to unlock hidden layers of umami and complexity, transforming grains and legumes into a full spectrum of flavours. Our journey reveals the traditional uses of koji in Japanese alcohol production and its innovative role in shaping modern mixology. While I strive to present koji's intricacies, I acknowledge its complexity and choose to highlight key elements to maintain clarity.

Next, we raise our glasses to sake. The centuries-old brewing process, regional variations, and diverse profiles of premium sake make it a subject of profound depth. To strike a balance between depth and simplicity, I provide a glimpse into the world of sake, focusing on its production and styles and their integration into contemporary cocktail creations.

Similarly, the book aims to celebrate the multifaceted spirit of shochu. Distilled from various raw materials, shochu's versatility exemplifies Japanese craftsmanship and creativity.

This exploration illuminates the stories behind distinct shochu varieties and their regional importance. While acknowledging shochu's complexities, I concentrate on key aspects to offer a comprehensive yet approachable understanding.

As our journey unfolds, we will encounter the fusion of Japan's drinking traditions with modern mixology. The book showcases iconic cocktails that pay homage to Japan's rich heritage while celebrating innovative cocktails that push the boundaries of creativity. Witness the seamless blending of koji, sake, and shochu with western spirits, guided by visionary bartenders from around the world.

In *The Art of Making Koji Cocktails*, I'll do my best to honour the legacy of Japan while celebrating the vibrant art of contemporary mixology. I'll present a refined and informative narrative, shedding light on the captivating spirits and sake of Japan.

Join me as I raise a toast to the rich cultural heritage that intertwines eastern alcohol production and western mixology.

CHAPTER TWO
KOJI

kōji 麹
/Kow-Jee/

1. "Koji is a mould that plays a crucial role in the
   production of various traditional Japanese alcoholic
   beverages, such as shochu, sake, and awamori. It is
   typically cultivated on rice, barley, or sweet potato."

To fully grasp the world of Japanese Sake and Shochu, you must first understand the importance of koji. At face value, Koji is nothing more than a fermentation aid, but Koji is so much more than that; it lies at the heart of most of Japan's indigenous food and drink production, performing more than just chemical processes. This unassuming mould holds the key to unlocking the exceptional flavours, unique aromas, and remarkable characteristics that make these traditional products cherished and celebrated worldwide.

When talking about koji, there are typically two words used: koji and koji-kin. Koji-kin refers more specifically to the mould itself, which is typically bought as a powder in Japan.

Koji-Kin is a specialised mould that thrives on rice, barley, and occasionally sweet potato, releasing essential enzymes that kickstart the saccharification process. This intricate process converts complex starches into simple sugars, similar to the malting of barley used in Scotch production. Understanding the true essence of koji opens the door to appreciating the art and science behind Japanese beverages.

The term "koji" is used as a general description for the product that results from impregnating a grain or tuber with koji-kin.

When koji-kin is grown on rice, it is called "koji," and the same applies when it's grown on sweet potatoes. Occasionally, you may see it specifically referred to as "rice koji" or "potato koji," but most commonly, it is simply referred to as "koji."

While it's fascinating to learn that there are many other types of Koji used in Japan for producing soy sauce, miso, as well as alcoholic beverages, we will focus solely on its role in alcohol production. Its true significance is often misunderstood, leading to misconceptions about its application. Contrary to common belief, Koji goes far beyond being just an enzymatic agent or cocktail ingredient.

In Japan, there exist specialised companies and research centres wholly devoted to comprehending and studying koji. While I will refrain from delving extensively into the scientific aspects concerning koji-kin, its life cycle, or any profoundly technical processes, I will lightly mention the key aspects relevant to alcohol production.

Koji's main role in alcohol production is saccharification, the process by which complex carbohydrates are broken down into sugars ready for alcohol fermentation.
In addition to this, it produces protease, an enzyme that transforms proteins into amino acids. It is these amino acids that give rise to the highly sought-after 'Umami' flavour, which adds a captivating depth to Sake and Shochu.

Koji-Kin comes in various strains; we typically use the colours of these strains to differentiate the type of Koji. But it's worth noting that each "colour" of Koji has a plethora of strains underneath it, which only the true nerds (or more likely producers such as shochu distillers and sake brewers) will take note of.

The three types commonly discussed for alcohol production are white, yellow, and black. As you can probably guess, white looks white, black looks black and yellow looks green. (Yes yellow koji can sometimes look more green than yellow in hue).

White koji is predominantly employed in shochu production, while black koji finds its place in the production of awamori. Sake, on the other hand, traditionally utilises yellow koji. While this colour-specific usage is not an absolute rule, it serves as a helpful guideline to remember when learning about these beloved Japanese drinks. However, it is becoming more common to see Japanese beverage producers exploring the uses of non-typical strains of Koji in their work.

In summary, Koji's significance goes far beyond simple saccharification. Its role in producing amino acids and infusing the beverages with the delightful 'Umami' flavour is what sets Japanese sake and shochu apart. Understanding and appreciating the uniqueness of koji will undoubtedly lead to a deeper appreciation for the rich cultural heritage and craftsmanship behind these traditional Japanese beverages.

Koji Types

Each type of koji outlined above has a different reason for being used, and understanding each will better help you understand the affects it has on a koji spirit or sake.

Here's a simple explanation of each type:

Yellow Koji (*a*spergillus *o*ryzae)

Derived from aspergillus oryzae, is primarily employed in the production of sake. It produces a rich umami driven liquid, sometimes fruity and refreshing, that is beloved by many.

White Koji (aspergillus kawachii)
White koji originated as a mutation from black koji in 1918. This variety is highly favoured for its ease of cultivation and the enzymes it contains, which promote rapid sugar conversion. Consequently, it has become widely used in the production of most shōchū today. The fermentation process involving white koji leads to the development of citric acid, imparting the resulting drink with a refreshing, mild, and sweet taste.

Black Koji (aspergillus awamori)
Black koji is used predominantly in the production of awamori. Like white koji, it also contributes to the development of citric acid, but the outcome is quite different. Black koji produces a robust and strongly flavoured shochu or sake. However, one of the challenges with using Black koji is that its spores spread very easily, making it difficult to completely clean away during the production process.

In hot regions such as Kyushu and Okinawa, there is higher microbiological activity. This increased activity poses a greater risk of fermentation spoilage. However, black and white koji, which produces citric acid, acts as a potent protector of fermentations. As a result, black and white koji strains are more preferable in these hot areas due to their ability to mitigate the risks associated with high temperatures and spoilage.

Below is an example of how you can incorporate of-the-shelf Koji into a modern cocktail.

In this cocktail, the Koji was used to break down the starches in a banana, releasing sugars and amino acids in the resulting juice.

Bananarama
Created by Samuel Boulton & Klára Kopčiková

20ml	Peanut Butter Cognac
20ml	Freya's Custard Cream Liqueur
20ml	Warninks Advocaat
50ml	Koji Banana Juice
3 Dash	Angostura Bitters
3 Dash	Saline

Glass:	Rocks
Method:	Shake & Strain
Ice:	Block
Garnish:	Peanut Brittle

Comments:
This drink was created for the The Pineapple Clubs 2022 Winter Cocktail menu.

Koji Banana Juice

675g	Peeled Banana (about 6)
135g	Kojimai (Rice Koji)
3g	Pectinase optional

Purée bananas then add to Vacuum bag with Koji and leave to infuse for 25 hours in the fridge.
After cook sous vide at 55 °C for three hours

Optional: Add Pectinase

Add Pectinase after cooking sous vide further thin and clarify the juice. Just add the Pectinase and let the juice rest at room temperature for an hour.

Finally filter with a mesh or cheese cloth to remove any remaining solids.

Peanut Butter Cognac

700ml	Cognac (we used Jules Gautret VS)
140g	100% Peanut Butter - Smooth

Add both ingredients to a container and stir until dissolved.

Other Koji Products

Although I said I would only discuss koji used for alcohol production, during the research for this book, I observed an obvious misunderstanding with koji (as described above) and a few other koji related products.

Shio Koji

Shio koji is a traditional Japanese ingredient used in cooking and food preparation. It is a mixture of salt, water, and rice koji (as mentioned above) and typically comes in liquid form.

Shio Koji is often used as a natural seasoning and tenderiser for various foods, including meats, fish, and vegetables. When applied to ingredients, it helps to enhance umami flavours, tenderise proteins, and reduce the overall cooking time. It is particularly popular in Japanese cuisine but has also gained recognition in other parts of the world for its unique culinary benefits.

Shio Koji is considered more of a culinary ingredient for cooking, rather than a beverage ingredient. While it can be seen in cocktails around the world, typically its used in a way which doesn't complement or enhance the taste of the cocktails. While experimenting with unconventional ingredients, understanding what you're mixing with is just as important. Shio Koji should be considered just like MSG or Salt in a cocktail, it's a flavour enhancer meant to expand the dimensions of a drink without adding too much of it's own flavour. One bartender who really understands this concept is renowned London bar tender Rueben Clark.

Banana | Fig Leaf
Created by Rueben Clark

40ml	Banana Infused Whiskey
15ml	Kanpai Sumi Sake
15ml	Fig Leaf Cordial
5ml	Koji Caramel

Glass:	Rocks
Method:	Stirred
Ice:	Block Ice
Garnish:	Fig Leaf Coin

Comments:
Originally created for a Takeover at Silverleaf in collaboration with Like Minded Creatures. However, due to its immense popularity the drink is reintroduce when fig leaves are in season.

Banana Infused Whiskey

750ml	Rye Whiskey
275g	Overripe bananas

Blend with pectinex, let sit for 24 hours before centrifuging at 4200rpm for 20 mins.

Fig Leaf Cordial

250ml	Filtered Water
150ml	Caster Sugar
13g	Fresh Fig Leaf
3g	Tartaric Acid

Blend on high and coffee filtered to remove solids.

Koji Caramel
Caramelise   500ml 2:1 Sugar Syrup
Add   200ml water and 50ml Shio Koji

Amazake
Amazake, is a delightful and traditional Japanese beverage that has been cherished for centuries. Derived from the words "ama" meaning sweet and "zake" signifying sake or alcohol, amazake translates to "sweet sake." However, despite the name, this nutritious drink contains little to no alcohol, making it a favourite among people of all ages.

Initially, it was used as an offering to the gods due to an association with prosperity and good fortune. Over time, its consumption expanded beyond religious contexts and became an integral part of everyday drinking, enjoyed by people in various settings, from street festivals to serene tea ceremonies.

The preparation of amazake involves cultivating rice with Yellow Koji (Aspergillus oryzae). The Koji breaks down the rice starches into natural sugars, giving rise to the drink's characteristic sweetness. While the traditional method involves a longer fermentation process, modern variations have been developed to offer a quicker and more accessible version.

Amazake boasts not only a delightful taste but also a multitude of health benefits. It is naturally rich in vitamins, minerals, and enzymes, making it an excellent source of nourishment. Many Japanese consider amazake a superfood, for its digestive properties.

In recent years, amazake has garnered attention beyond Japan's borders, gaining popularity in the global wellness and vegan communities. Its versatility has led to innovative uses, such as incorporating it into desserts, smoothies, and even skincare products.

Amazake's subtle sweetness and creamy texture can be served hot or cold, and of course, can be mixed into a cocktail.

Amazake Swizzle
Created by Austin Hennelly

60ml	Swizzle Batch
30ml	Orgeat
22.5ml	Fresh Lime Juice
30ml	Chinotto Soda

Glass:	Highball
Method:	Swizzle
Ice:	Crushed
Garnish:	Lime Zest and Grated Nutmeg

Swizzle Batch
960ml	Chai Concentrate
810ml	Coconut Milk
430ml	Amazake

Add all of the swizzle batch ingredients to a large vessel that can seal and mix together. It will keep in the refrigerator for a week.

Sake Kasu
While Sake kasu isn't a form of Koji, it is made using Koji, it can also be a great ingredient to cocktails if used correctly.

Sake kasu, also known as "sake lees", is a byproduct of the sake-making process. During the sake production process, the rice and other ingredients are fermented to produce alcohol, and the solid residue that remains after the pressing are called sake kasu.
Japan has a long history of using left over ingredients to make new products, later we'll discuss Kasutori Shochu which is made using sake kasu in Japan. Outside Japan, if you want to buy the solids, you can get them for free, or cheaply from a Sake producer, or frozen from a Japanese food supplier.

Sake kasu has several culinary uses and is valued for its unique flavour and nutritional properties.

Here are some common uses for sake kasu:
Cooking: Sake kasu can be used as a seasoning or marinade in various Japanese dishes. It imparts a mild, umami-rich flavour. It's particularly popular in miso soup and grilled dishes.

Pickling: Sake kasu can be used to make pickles, such as "sake kasu-zuke." It's mixed with salt and other seasonings to create a flavourful brine for pickling vegetables or fish.

Desserts: In some desserts, sake kasu is used to add a subtle sweetness and complexity. For example, it can be incorporated into ice creams, custards, or confectionary.

Beverages: It can also be used to make drinks like amazake, but can also be used directly into modern cocktails like the below.

Miami Rice
Created by Brian Evans

45ml	Beniotome Sesame Shochu
15ml	Cardinal Spirits Tiki Rum
5ml	Rhum Clément Mahina Coco
30ml	Sake Kasu Syrup
15ml	Pineapple Juice
15ml	Cucumber Juice
7.5ml	Lime Juice
180g	Crushed Ice
60ml	Float on top Strawberry Daiquiri Purée

Glass:	Open Top Glass.
Method:	Blended
Ice:	None
Garnish:	None

Comments:
This drink was first featured in a Punch article on punchdrink.com

Sake Kasu Syrup
400g	White granulated sugar
400g	Hot water
50g	Sake Kasu
8g	Salt

Add all ingredients to a blender and blend until smooth. Do not strain. Refrigerated, for up to 2 weeks.

Strawberry Daiquiri Purée

750g	Strawberries
250g	Sugar
50ml	Wray and Nephew Jamaican Rum
2g	Malic acid
2g	Citric acid

Remove tops of strawberries and cut into quarters.
Add all ingredients to a blender and blend until smooth. Do not strain. Refrigerated, for up to 2 weeks.

Koji Outside of Japan

While our primary focus will be on Koji and its uses in Japan, I thought it advantageous to briefly discuss Koji outside of Japan. In the world of alcohol, one prominent player that comes to mind is Empirical.

Established in 2017 by Lars Williams and Mark Emil Hermansen, their motto has become 'Flavour has no boundaries.' To say they engage in out-of-the-box thinking is an understatement.

Below is a discussion with Lars Williams, the Copenhagen-based former director of the Nordic Food Lab and now co-owner of Empirical Spirits, about their ethos regarding the Koji spirits they produce.

Can you start by explaining what Koji you use at Empirical and in what forms?

We've been using Aspergillus Oryzae from the start, with a focus on pearled barley (60% polished) as part of our original grain bill. We also experimented at the outset with Aspergillus Luchuensis, but its heightened acidic flavour profile didn't translate as well as we had hoped, as citric acid is too heavy to be distilled. Regarding other substrates, we've pretty much tried to cultivate Aspergillus Oryzae on everything we could get our hands on, including manioc from the Brazilian Amazon for a future limited edition release or parsnip for a spirit we never launched.

We've also gone beyond the enzymatic function in our production cycle and showcased barley koji as a botanical in its own right. Two limited editions come to mind: Bandit and Onyx. Cold-smoked barley-koji was the sole botanical in Bandit, bringing forth potent umami flavours of fresh mushrooms and a creamy mouthfeel. We created Onyx specifically for Lyaness in London. One of the main botanicals in this blend was black koji. Once our barley koji was ready, we blackened it as you would garlic through a lengthy Maillard reaction. This process added some very chocolate-forward flavours to the sweet floral layers of Aspergillus Oryzae.

While we were further examining our production cycle, we explored new uses for our koji-forward spent grain. With circularity in mind, we created a line of provisions featuring some shoyu and miso-like products, repurposing our spent grain and smoked koji to create new flavour experiences to share. There are enough koji experiments in our minds to last us a lifetime.

What led Empirical to explore the use of Koji in the production of their spirits?

Throughout my career in kitchens and at the Nordic Food Lab, I was very familiar with koji-making and used it extensively as a flavour enhancer. I spent a long time in Japan, learning the technique from the best, delving into its endless flavour possibilities while paying respect to the century-long traditions. It only seemed natural that koji would be an intrinsic part of what we did at Empirical. We created Empirical in 2017 to shape a future for flavour that is delicious, impactful, and beyond the obvious. We are continually inspired by the role flavour plays in our ability to create and transport experiences. Spirits were our first step in sharing these sensory memories. With flavour as our North Star, it was imperative for us to do everything from scratch, from grain to bottle, and build new flavour layers at each step of our process, starting with koji.
While also using Pilsner malt as a raw ingredient for our brew, we also wanted to extract the incredibly soft floral, umami, and tropical notes of koji, while benefiting from its enzymatic 'powers' for our ferments. We retain these elegant estery and polyphenolic notes through vacuum distillation, resulting in a very flavour-forward spirit as a base for our botanical macerations.

What types of spirits is Empirical producing using Koji, and how does the use of Koji differentiate them from traditional spirit production?

In the first couple of years at Empirical, our barley koji/Pilsner malt grain bill was used as a base for all our spirits. As we constantly strive to make each batch better than the last, we realised that each spirit needed its own individual grain bill, designed to elevate its respective botanicals. Among our current products, only "The Plum, I Suppose" still has barley koji as a base. The soft flavours of the koji highlight the floral and fruity aromas of our botanicals, namely plum kernels and marigold petals.

What are some of the key challenges you've encountered when incorporating Koji into your production process?

We had to completely redesign our processes, and, more importantly, our equipment. To be able to steam up to 400kg of dry pearled barley, we repurposed a 70-year-old butter churner from Jutland, Denmark. It allows us to soak, strain, and steam the grain in the same receptacle. The churner's drum rotates as we steam, keeping the barley loose and evenly cooked. We custom-built a koji muro, all lined with Douglas Fir Wood, and designed our koji bed to allow sufficient airflow to control the temperature of our grain during the growth process.
Some adjustments needed to be made in our brew system as well. A regular mash tun setup uses a dry mill for the malt, but we had to substitute it with a wet hammer mill due to the texture of our koji. The same thing applied to the mash filter. We had to install a hydraulic pressure mash filter instead of using a false bottom in our mash tun to separate our solids from our wort, as the mashed koji had a porridge-like consistency, acting like glue on the perforated plaque.

Could you elaborate on the specific benefits that Koji brings to the production of spirits?

It brings incredible layers of flavour while being a great tool for very versatile fermentations.

Again, the possibilities for flavour exploration are endless.

Are there any environmental or sustainability advantages to using Koji in your production process?

There are no advantages to using koji when it comes to sustainability. In fact, there is no such thing as a sustainable distillery, as you always need electricity, water, and manpower. Nevertheless, it is interesting to approach production with a circular mindset and continuously question what we do and how we can make it better. How can we find new flavour applications beyond the first production cycle? What can we do with what some call 'production waste' and turn it into a new product? This is how we started our provisions line.

If you do Multiple Parallel Fermentation, how does this differ from traditional fermenting?

We don't perform multiple parallel fermentations, but we have been working with a number of different ways to incorporate koji into brewing over the years. As our processes evolved, we stopped mashing our pilsner malt and koji together. Instead, we now start by creating a kind of amazake with our barley koji and add it to our malted barley and Belgian Saison yeast fermentation. Shifting to this technique improved the extraction of koji flavours in our low wine.

Are there any specific safety or quality control measures you've had to implement due to the use of Koji in your production?

As mentioned above, we built our own koji muro with a 14 Pascal positive pressure system and HEPA filters. Before entering the koji muro, the staff goes through a first entry lock with 7 Pascals of pressure, ensuring that we constantly force the air out of the koji room. Naturally, we implement rigorous sanitation protocols, and our staff wears koji-specific shoes. As mentioned before, we lined our koji muro with untreated Douglas Fir wood, which possesses the same antibacterial properties as traditional cedar wood in Japan.

How do you source and maintain the Koji cultures for your spirits production?

We buy our koji-kin directly from Japan. Having our own culture is a dream of ours, and we conducted initial trials. We managed to maintain the strain for the first 20 generations, but we realised that we could not achieve the expected results and consistency beyond 3 generations. Considering the volumes we were producing, we needed a potent and reliable strain.

Could you share any insights on the consumer reception and market demand for spirits produced using Koji?

I believe there is a growing interest and demand for koji-based products. It has certainly gained popularity through its culinary applications in some of the best restaurants in the world. It seems that people started to discover what koji was, even though they certainly enjoyed it in shoyu, miso, or sake in the past. They just didn't know it.
In Denmark, in particular, the natural wine movement has popularised high-quality sake as a pairing option as well as a standalone drink. Shochu will likely be the next to follow.

People can now finally put a name to what they had already tasted. However, instead of the mass-produced and lower-quality products they consumed, they now look for premium and high-quality products, with flavour nuances as a priority.

What is your vision for the future of Empirical and the use of Koji in spirits production?

As I mentioned, at the moment, only "The Plum, I Suppose" has a koji base, but we are still exploring new applications, including a future limited release.
We are excited to see the growing interest in koji-making and fermentation as a whole. There is an increasing awareness of all the wonderful flavour nuances and complexity that koji brings to your drinks. We are excited to see more sake, shochu, and other uncategorised spirits in bar drink programs.

Can you discuss any ongoing research or development efforts to further optimise the use of Koji in your production process?

As mentioned previously, we optimised our use of koji by creating a new product line from spent grains. We always like to quote the very talented chef and friend Matt Orlando, who says, "There's no such thing as a by-product; it's just another product."
We also continue to research other cultures' approaches to koji or similar Aspergillus strains like Brasiliensis in Brazil, for example, as well as its various applications in countries such as China and Korea. Flavour knows no boundaries, so how can we learn from them and further explore and share these experiences?

How do you educate consumers and the industry about the benefits and uniqueness of Koji-based spirits?

At the Copenhagen distillery, we conducted tours and tastings, during which we showed our guests how it was done, and sometimes even while it was being done, giving them a chance to taste barley koji in its pure form.
We also created a series of educational videos on our social media channels that walked through our koji production process step by step.
But at the end of the day, I believe that the real test is to get people to taste spirits with and without koji side by side, without any botanicals. That's where they can truly experience the depth and nuances of koji.

Lastly, what advice would you give to bartenders interested in exploring Koji spirits as an ingredient in their cocktails?

Have fun. Color outside the lines and explore beyond the obvious. Only flavours matter.

Koji Terminology

Koji (麹)
Refers to rice or other grains that have been cultivated with the Koji mould.

Koji-kin (麹菌)
The specific strain/spore used for cultivating Koji.

Kome-Koji (米麹)
Koji made from rice, the most common type used in Japan.

Mugi-Koji (麦麹)
Koji made from barley, used in some regional varieties of shochu.

Aspergillus Oryzae
The primary mould strain used in Koji fermentation of Sake production, often referred to as Yellow Koji

Aspergillus Kawachii
A mutation of Aspergillus Awamori (Black Koji). The primary mould strain used in Koji fermentation of Shochu production, often referred to as White Koji.

Aspergillus Awamori
The primary mould strain used in Koji fermentation of Awamori, production, often referred to as Black Koji. Know to stain items is comes into contact with black.

Amylases
A type of enzyme produced by Koji mould that breaks down starches into sugars like maltose and glucose.

Proteases
Enzymes that break down proteins into smaller peptides and amino acids during the Koji fermentation process.

CHAPTER THREE
PRE LEARNING

Welcome to the "Pre-Learning" chapter of our exploration into Koji, Sake and Shochu. Here, I recognise that the world of these drinks can be as complex and nuanced as any other. I've designed this section to provide you with a solid grounding before we delve deeper into the specifics of each alcohol's production and history. Think of it as the cornerstone upon which I will build your understanding. This section might seem a bit 'all over the place' initially, but please bear with me!

I appreciate that these topics might seem rudimentary or obvious to some readers, and some I go into intense detail so this chapter is flexible. It is entirely modular, allowing you to read it in sequential order or pick and choose topics you want to explore. There's no need to worry about missing out on essential knowledge. If, at any point later in the book, you find yourself in need of a better understanding of certain terms or concepts, you can always return to this chapter as a valuable reference.

Umami

Umami is one of the five basic tastes, alongside sweet, sour, salty, and bitter. It is often described as a savoury or meaty taste however I think this is down to pour understanding as we see this taste in many foods that aren't savoury or meat, I prefer to described it as a richness.

The term "umami" comes from the Japanese words "umai," which means delicious, and "mi," which means taste. It was first identified and named by Japanese chemist Kikunae Ikeda in the early 20th century.

Umami taste is primarily associated with certain amino acids, especially glutamate and to some extent aspartate. These compounds are naturally present in a variety of foods and play a crucial role in creating the characteristic umami flavour. Some common sources of umami include:

Glutamate: Glutamate is the most well-known and prominent amino acid responsible for the umami flavour. It is found in foods like ripe tomatoes, aged cheeses (e.g., Parmesan), and various proteins (meat and fish), contributing to their savoury taste.

Aspartate: Aspartate is another amino acid that can contribute to the umami taste, although it is generally glutamate that is most strongly associated with this flavour.

Inosinate and Guanylate: These nucleotide compounds can enhance the umami taste when combined with glutamate-rich ingredients. For example, monosodium glutamate (MSG), a common umami-enhancing food additive, contains glutamate and can be combined with inosinate and guanylate to amplify the savoury taste in dishes.

Umami is an essential element in culinary traditions around the world, and it plays a significant role in enhancing the overall taste and depth of many dishes. When combined with other tastes like sweetness, sourness, saltiness, and bitterness, umami can create a complex and satisfying profile in various foods and recipes.

Geographical Indication
A geographical indication (GI) is an intellectual property right used for products with qualities or characteristics that can be attributed to a specific geographical origin. The World Trade Organization have awarded numerous geographical indicators to Shochu. While Japan recognises many other geographical indicators for sake and shochu, internally. As we progress through the book, I will discuss all the shochu indicators as they come up. However, I will refrain from discussing the sake geographical indicators. The reason for this is that geographical indicators in sake are relatively new, and currently, many new indicators are being approved each year.

While writing this book, two new indicators have been approved, so any information printed on this may quickly become outdated. If you want up to date information on Japan's geographical indicators please head to the National Tax Agency of Japan's website.

Sake Temperature
Sake is hugely versatile, not only in styles and gradings but also in the intricate relationship between its temperature and flavour. Much like a symphony conductor, there is a balance to be made. The temperature at which sake is enjoyed can significantly influence its fragrance, body, and taste. Unfortunately, in the West, we have this idea that sake is served hot or that "cheap sake is served hot." While there are elements that have affected these statements, neither of these statements is 100% correct. The temperature you enjoy your sake at is up to you; that's it. While some sake may have been designed to be consumed chilled or warm, it is best to simply drink it how you enjoy it.

Generally speaking, sake is warmed in order to enhance certain flavours or elements. Amino acids present in all sake are more easily identifiable on our tongues at different temperatures, meaning some sakes benefit from being warmed or chilled. However, there is no one-size-fits-all rule, simply some fundamental principles to consider to understand the impact that temperature can have on sake.

Chilling vs. Warming
The temperature at which you serve sake can either enhance or mute its fragrance. Over-chilling sake tends to suppress its aroma, while warming it can intensify the fragrance, though not always favourably.

Alcohol Perception
Heating sake can heighten your perception of its alcohol content, both in terms of its aroma and on the palate. Again, in some sake, this can be pleasant, but in others, it can be overpowering.

Sweetness and Dryness
The same sake served at different temperatures can taste either drier or sweeter. Cold temperatures accentuate dryness, while warmth brings out sweetness.

Flavour Balance
Temperature adjustments can significantly impact the balance of flavours. Colder temperatures tend to favour fruity and light flavours, while warming sake brings forward rice, mushroom, and umami notes.

Armed with these basic principles, we can begin to understand why certain sakes are better suited to specific temperature ranges.

Matching Sake Types with Temperatures
Different categories of sake lend themselves to particular temperature ranges, but there are always exceptions. Here's a rough guide:

Daiginjo and Ginjo
These sake types, characterised by delicate fragrances and flavours, are generally best served at colder temperatures (4°C-15°C). Extreme cold, however, may mute their subtleties.

Junmai
Junmai sake offers versatility, ranging from cold (4°C-15°C) to room temperature (21°C) and even warm (29°C-46°C).

Honjozo
Honjozo sake, can be enjoyed cold (4°C-15°C), at room temperature (21°C), warm (29°C-46°C), or even hot (49°C and above). Explore the extremes to discover the bottle's full character.

Futsushu
Table sake, or futsushu, exhibits a wide variety of flavours and textures. While some shine when served cold, most can withstand varying degrees of heat.

Nigori
Nigori sake is at its best when served cold (4°C-15°C), and some varieties can be enjoyed over ice (below 4°C). Its creamy

texture is most pronounced at lower temperatures. However, there are many examples of this style I enjoy warm.

Sparkling
Sparkling sake, known for its full body and lower alcohol content, is best enjoyed chilled (4°C-15°C) to maintain its crispness.

How to Warm Sake

For those who prefer their sake warmed, there are traditional and modern methods to achieve the desired temperature. In Japan, they have a sake setting on their microwave as it's so common; however, I can't imagine a traditional Toji likes the idea of this. One traditional approach is the hot bath method:

Pour the sake into a suitable vessel, such as a Japanese decanter known as a "tokkuri."
Submerge the tokkuri in a pot of water, ensuring that the liquid level inside the tokkuri matches that of the water in the pot.

Gradually heat the pot, akin to melting chocolate or butter, using a stove.

Alternatively, you can submerge the tokkuri in water that has already been boiled, allowing it to cool slightly before immersing the sake bottle or tokkuri. Be cautious not to put a very cold bottle into boiling water, as it may cause the glass to break. Use room-temperature vessels for safety.

How to Determine the Best Temperature

A method I learned from Tengu Sake's director, Oliver Hilton-Johnson. Heat your sake up via your preferred method to a hot temperature (almost too hot to drink). Put in a thermometer, taste, and write down notes. As the temperature drops, try every few degrees, recording your notes and preferences until the sake is back at room temperature. Do the same from very cold to room temperature. This was the method we employed at my sake bar, Shibuya Underground, for every sake.

Water

Sake comprises just four natural elements: rice, water, yeast, and koji. Each of these components plays a vital role in shaping the flavour of sake, but one ingredient reigns supreme: water. In the final product, sake consists of roughly 80-85% water, underscoring the pivotal role that water quality plays in sake production. Throughout the brewing process, more than fifty times the weight of rice is consumed in water. Not only does water contribute to the final taste and ABV adjustment, but it is also instrumental in washing, soaking, and steaming the rice before fermentation begins. Unquestionably, excellent sake owes its greatness to exceptional water, making it imperative to understand what constitutes ideal water for sake production.

The flavour and texture of water is significantly influenced by minerals like calcium, magnesium, and calcium carbonate, categorising water as either "soft" or "hard" based on its mineral content. High mineral content defines "hard" water, while "soft" water has a low mineral concentration. Japanese water, in particular, is renowned for its exceptional softness compared to waters from other famous water regions of the world. Soft water is great for the sake brewing process, and

Japan's abundant supply of it has rendered the country a perfect hub for sake production.

Another factor adding to Japan's amazing water is its topography. Japan sits on or near the boundary of four tectonic plates: the Pacific, North American, Eurasian, and Filipino plates. This means Japan has mountains- and a lot of them. In fact, Japan has over 100 active volcanoes (including the famous Mt. Fuji). For those in the water world, this is great news. Mountain landscapes can function like natural sponges. Porous rock formations, such as limestone and sandstone, can absorb and store water like a sponge. These rocks have small openings and fractures that can temporarily retain water, allowing it to slowly seep into underground aquifers. This slow release of water helps regulate downstream flow and filter out impurities. These underground water sources are often fed by precipitation that percolates through the mountains, slowly filtering out impurities and pollutants. The stored groundwater can then emerge as clean, natural springs many years later.

Aquifer water is typically high in potassium, phosphoric acid, and magnesium, which are indispensable in yeast propagation within the starter (shubo) and the development of koji in rice. Insufficient quantities of these can hinder yeast multiplication, influencing the entire fermentation process. This is why historically the biggest area for sake production was Nada - Hyogo, which has famously hard water (for Japan) and was able to make sustainable and safe fermentations. More on this later.

Soft water is also great for brewing, however requires different techniques than hard water. I will mention these techniques later in this book, but they are connected to the mineral content of the water.

Not all minerals are good for sake. Water containing iron and manganese proves unsuitable, even detrimental, to sake production. The presence of iron can darken the sake and negatively impact its aroma and flavour.

So, in essence, great sake water is water that contains adequate potassium, phosphoric acid, and magnesium while remaining free from iron and manganese contamination. Now you understand this, it should come as no surprise that most sake breweries in Japan are strategically located near abundant sources of pristine water, such as rivers, mountains, or underground wells.

Miyamizu
While most of Japan has great water, there is one area that won the lottery and is regarded as the best. This water can be found in the Nada region of Kobe, Hyogo prefecture. This water, known as Miyamizu was discovered by Tazaemon Yamamura towards the end of the Edo period (1603 - 1868). Tazaemon's epiphany occurred after building a second brewery. He observed that one brewery produced sake that always surpassed the quality of the other. After trial and error, they identified water as the sole differentiating factor. Tazaemon promptly declared Miyamizu as superior. Subsequently, many breweries vied for access to this renowned water, with specialised water vendors even making it available nationwide.

Miyamizu boasts elevated levels of phosphorus and potassium, serving as nourishment for koji and yeast, in turn promoting enzyme activity. Miyamizu also exhibits minimal iron content, rendering it one of Japan's premier sake waters.

Cocktail History of Japan

The opening of Japan by Commodore Matthew Perry in 1854 threw the country into chaos and the early days of western involvement in Japan was nothing like the civilised experiences of later years.

Post-WW2, the Japanese bartending community professionalised under guilds dotted throughout the country. Just as with other crafts, apprentices learned (what is now called international bartending) under the watchful eye of their mentors and masters, who were every bit as strict as in other disciplines. Today hundreds of cocktail bars throughout Japan can trace their roots to proteges of these post-war pioneers.

Japan isn't a cocktail culture like we think in of the west. Cocktails are associate with a Western experience like hotel bars, and restaurant bars, most restaurants in Japan don't have bars incorporated into them. In Japan it's quite common for people to order the same drinks, all having beer together for example. However in the west cocktail are more individual, with each person choosing what best fits them.

The style of Japanese bartending most commonly seen today, came from the high-end cruise ships and grand hotels on the late 1950/60's, these bartenders are almost always clothed a tuxedo or at least a bow tie and were nearly always men. The first cocktails served in Japan were in western hotels catering to foreign businessmen, then later to entertain tourists for the first time. The Japanese took this experience and spent decades perfecting it, ironing out every detail from clothing, to glassware and of course clear ice. Some Japanese cocktails bars now are like a time machine to these 1960's luxury "international" bars.

Japanese cocktails bars for a long time were for salarymen to finalise business meetings or impress clients, they didn't want to party, or to be bothered with long speeches of ingredients. This means drinks can be made one at a time, perfectly, with care, speed was never the priority, the impressiveness of the process and craft is what they are after.

Ironically as Japan protected this style, the rest of the world moved on to party bars, sour mix and blue drinks, so much in fact, as the west moved back to the idea of quality and fresh, Japans bar style rose to fame, with bartenders around the world idolising the theology they'd held, but forgotten.

Pro tip: When you go to a bar in Japan, order you first drink, when it arrives order another. Speed is not the aim for the majority of bars in Japan, so it will take a while to arrive.

When talking about classic Japanese cocktails, they're not many to discuss. However, a few drinks do come to mind:

The Bamboo
The Bamboo cocktail holds a unique and significant place in the history of cocktails in Japan. While its origins have been attributed to "some Englishman" in the Western Kansas World on September 11, 1886, it is widely regarded as one of the earliest cocktails to be crafted in Japan and is still enjoyed by many today. While it's possible that the Bamboo cocktail did

not originate in Japan, its popularisation in the country is credited to Louis Eppinger, a talented barman of German descent.

Eppinger's journey to Japan was notable; he was imported from the USA in 1889 to the Grand Hotel in Yokohama with a mission to establish a Western-style bar culture at the hotel. It is believed that the Bamboo cocktail found its place on the menu there around 1890, under Eppinger.

More than a century later, the Bamboo cocktail continues to be savoured, serving as a testament to its enduring appeal and the indelible mark it has left on Japanese cocktail culture. Its rich history reflects the fusion of international influences and the lasting legacy of Japan's love for the art of mixology.

45ml	French Vermouth
45ml	Sherry
2 Dash	Orange Bitters

Glass:	Stemmed Cocktail Glass
Method:	Stirred
Ice:	Cracked ice
Garnish:	Lemon Peel

The Japanese Cocktail

The inception of the first *Japanese cocktail* holds a bizarre historical twist. Surprisingly, this cocktail was not created in Japan and didn't embody Japanese culture in any significant manner. It was the brainchild of the legendary Jerry Thomas, Thomas created it in 1860 as a tribute to the arrival of the first Japanese diplomatic mission to the United States.

Prior to this diplomatic mission, which included dignitaries adorned with samurai swords in traditional dress, there was no notable Japanese presence in the United States. Meaning, the ingredients in the drink have no tangible Japanese inspiration.

Tokyo-based cocktail historian Kadzuo Ishizura's perspective on this is that Jerry Thomas may have been attempting to replicate the flavours of Chinese Shaoxing wine (a type of rice wine from Shaoxing, a city in China's Zhejiang Province). It's possible, as the USA did have a significant presence of Chinese immigrants during that era, which could have exposed Thomas to Shaoxing wine. This shows the low level of understanding for Asian cultures during this time but further exemplifies how the world of mixology, even in its early days, was shaped by cross-cultural exchange!

Ingredients:

60ml	Brandy
15ml	Orgeat syrup
2.5ml	Bogarts bitters

Glass:	Stemmed Cocktail Glass
Method:	Stirred
Ice:	Cracked ice

Garnish: Lemon Peel

Sosogi-Koboshi - The Famous Overspill Pour
When you order a single glass of sake, the server might present you with an empty glass nestled within a masu, which there server then proceed to pour sake until it overflows, with the masu serving as a vessel to capture any excess liquid. This manner of serving is referred to as "sosogi-koboshi," a term combining the verbs "sosogu" (to pour) and "kobosu" (to spill over). Although this method of filling the glass doesn't carry any specific symbolism, it is widely perceived as a symbol of generosity to pour until the glass overflows, giving you extra.
There is no real etiquette on how to drink this, which many articles online would have you believe, drink however you'd like. From the cup, the masu, whichever you'd like. Just spill as little as possible!

Multiple Parallel Fermentation
In the conventional alcohol-making process, starches are typically converted into sugars before commencing alcohol fermentation. This can involve methods like malting for whiskey or utilising a ready liquid sugar source like molasses for rum production.
However, in the case of Koji, it breaks down the starches present in solid grains such as barley or rice into simpler sugars, including glucose. These sugars then serve as the substrate for yeast during the subsequent conversion into alcohol.
What sets multiple parallel fermentation apart is its simultaneous occurrence of both these processes, which stands as a defining characteristic of Japanese alcohol production. Due to these processes happening at the same time, multiple

parallel fermentation ferments, tend to be lengthier compared to standard alcohol fermentations.

Japanese Historical Periods Timeline
I've included a small timeline here as a reference for later in the book, as I will mention various periods (such as Meiji and Edo) multiple times.

Heian Period (794 CE - 1185 CE):
Capital moved to Heian-kyo (modern-day Kyoto).
Development of courtly culture
Rise of the samurai class.

Kamakura Period (1185 CE - 1333 CE):
Minamoto no Yoritomo establishes the Kamakura Shogunate.
The samurai class gains prominence.

Muromachi Period (1336 CE - 1573 CE):
The Ashikaga Shogunate comes to power.
Onin War (1467-1477) leads to the Warring States period (Sengoku Jidai).

Azuchi-Momoyama Period (1573 CE - 1603 CE):
Oda Nobunaga and Toyotomi Hideyoshi unify Japan.
Construction of impressive castles.
Introduction of Christianity by Portuguese missionaries.

Edo Period (1603 CE - 1868 CE):
Tokugawa Ieyasu establishes the Tokugawa Shogunate.
Period of peace and stability known as the "Edo Peace."
Strict isolationist policies, such as sakoku, are implemented.

Meiji Period (1868 CE - 1912 CE):
Emperor Meiji restores imperial power.
Modernisation and Westernisation of Japan's political, economic, and social systems.
Abolition of the samurai class and feudalism.

Taisho Period (1912 CE - 1926 CE):
Japan's participation in World War I and the Treaty of Versailles.
Emergence of a democratic political system.

Showa Period (1926 CE - 1989 CE):
Expansionist policies lead to Japan's involvement in World War II.
The atomic bombings of Hiroshima and Nagasaki.
Post-war reconstruction.

Heisei Period (1989 CE - 2019 CE):
Emperor Akihito's reign.
Economic stagnation and recovery.
Japan becomes a major player in the global economy.

Reiwa Period (2019 CE - Present):
Emperor Naruhito's reign.

This timeline provides an overview of Japan's major historical periods, from its ancient beginnings to the present day|}. Each era brought significant changes to Japan's culture, politics, and society.

CHAPTER FOUR
SAKE

Nihonshu
/Ni-Hon-Shu/

1. A Japanese alcoholic beverage fermented from polished rice commonly called Sake.

Sake Introduction

For individuals unfamiliar with sake or who have not had the opportunity to visit Japan, it may come as a surprise that the proper term for this beverage is Nihonshu.

"Nihon" (日本) translates to Japan, while "Shu" (酒) translates to alcohol.

The literal translation of Nihonshu would be Japanese-Alcohol

It is essential to note that Kanji, the logographic characters used in the Japanese writing system, can be read in two ways: independently and within a sentence. For instance, the Kanji for "alcohol" (酒) can be read as "Shu" when used in conjunction with other characters, and as "Sake" when standing alone.

In the context of Japanese language, "sake" refers to alcohol in general. However, it is important to understand that while all alcohol in Japan can be referred to as "sake," only what we consider sake is called Nihonshu.

Despite this distinction, the term "sake" is commonly used worldwide, and for consistency, it shall be referred to as such throughout this book.

Sake Introduction

Sake is a multi-faceted category with more information than any one person could write in a book. Through this book, I will do my best to simplify the world of sake while retaining the necessary information in usable and interesting forms.

Sake production has been around since before recorded history. It is believed to have started somewhere around 500 BC in China. As with many things, this alcohol made its way over to Japan where the practice was developed and refined into the cultural phenomenon we know today.

Sake is often simply decried as 'rice wine.' However, I find it hard expressing my reservations about this phrase, I find it fails to encompass the full depth of sake's significance. Beyond being a mere beverage, sake holds a profound place within Japanese culture, seamlessly woven into the fabric of everyday life, be it at an Izakaya or the grandeur of prestigious ceremonies and cultural gatherings.

There are many ways to make sake, and each sake brewery and Toji (master brewer) has their own philosophy on sake's production and what the end result should be. Dilution by one brewery may be seen as essential, whereas another brewery may not believe in diluting their sake at all.

I will be breaking down sake to its bare elements in the book; however, I will not be able to cover everything. After this book, should you wish to know more, please seek out a course such as a WSET to continue your learning.

Production

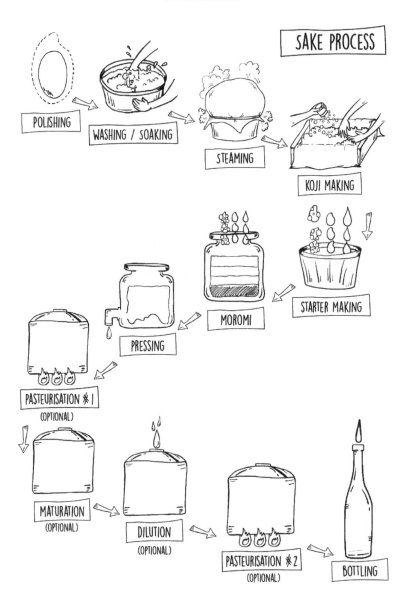

This graphic provides a concise overview of sake production. Please note that it is a simplified guide and does not cover all the steps involved in detail. Additionally, some steps, such as the second pasteurisation, can be conducted in tanks but are often performed in bottles.

Rice Selection, Growing, and Harvesting

Sake production begins with the cultivation of rice, normally, specialist sake rice. This rice is larger than the type used for consumption and requires careful nurturing. It grows from spring to summer and is harvested between late August and late September. Different regions have their unique varieties of sake rice. Sake rice has been bred over many years and is noticeably different from table rice it resembles an egg, with two distinct layers; the centre, called the shimpaku, contains starch, and the outer layer, called the endosperm, is made up of vitamins, minerals, and proteins. It grows larger and rounder than table rice, with higher starch content and lower protein levels. Specially cultivated in specific growing conditions, it is essential for premium sake production, with varieties like Yamadanishiki and Gohyakumangoku being popular choices among brewers. Table rice, on the other hand, is grown for general consumption and varies in size, shape, and starch content, with higher protein levels, and is used as a staple food but can also be used for sake production.

The amount of Sake rice strains in Japan is continually evolving, with crossbreeding and genetic modification being a common practice to create newer and improved strains which make great sake. Another reason for this work is due to climate change, colder regions are now able to cultivate strains that were not typically viable there before and warm regions are seeing changes in their growing, and harvesting cycles.

Fun Fact:
Some ancestral strains, such as Omachi, cannot grow in soil when combined with modern fertilisers. Therefore, farms use crushed oyster shells in the fields as a natural fertiliser.

Rice Milling
Once harvested, the rice goes through a crucial milling process. Modern rice milling machines are used to control the polishing ratio, speed, and temperature, but human judgment remains essential. The goal is to remove the outer layers of the rice to reach its core starch, resulting in elegant aromas. Machines can polish away as little as 1% or as much as 99%. Polishing isn't a fast process, and the later can take many months to get to.

Washing and Soaking
The milled rice is then washed and soaked to achieve the perfect level of moisture needed for steaming. This step is monitored with precision, and premium Ginjo-grade sake involves hand washing in small batches, following the traditional method. To be as precise as they need, using modern stopwatches is necessary.

Steaming
Steaming the rice is the first task at the sake brewery each morning. It is steamed for a specific duration to achieve a balance of firmness on the outside and softness on the inside. The Sake maker checks the rice's readiness by shaping a small round cake in their palm and sometimes by tasting.

Koji Making

Koji, as mentioned, is a crucial component in sake production and is made via a meticulous two-day process. The sake maker cultivates koji-kin onto steamed rice. The koji mould works its way into the rice grains and releases enzymes that convert starch into sugar, a necessary step for fermentation.

The Yeast Starter (Shubo)

The yeast starter, also known as shubo, is a concentrated fermentation starter. It consists of koji, steamed rice, water, and yeast. This step is to create a healthy population of yeast able to complete fermentation. In traditional/ancient methods, this step would also start the production of lactic acid which protects the brewing process from foreign contamination. Modern methods use commercially produced lactic acid.

The Mash

The shubo is transferred into a larger tank or vat, where rice, koji, and water are added over the course of 4 days. This marks the main fermentation process, which takes around 3 to 4 weeks. The temperature is closely monitored and adjusted throughout this period. At the end of the fermentation process, this is where the producer has the decision to add distilled alcohol. (more on this later)

Side note: The addition of alcohol here is not the same as fortification in Vermouth production. The addition of alcohol will halt the fermentation and also dry the resulting sake, but has nothing to do with additional ABV, as most sake will be diluted down to a similar drinking strength regardless of whether alcohol is added or not.

Pressing

After fermentation is complete, the newly born sake is separated from the solid remains of the fermented rice. Higher graded sake, such as Daiginjo, might use a traditional press machine or a cotton bag. However, modern sake breweries often use a gentle press machine to extract the sake. Some sake makers may skip this step and opt for a mesh filter mentioned next. Depending on the level of pressing, this is where the brew can choose to make a cloudy sake known as "Nigori".

Filtering

The sake then undergoes filtering or fining. This can be in the form of a steel mesh filter if you want to keep the product cloudy or a fine powdered active carbon can be used to remove unwanted colour and flavours. Some sake makers are now opting to skip this step, creating unfined sake known as 'Muroka'.

Pasteurisation

To preserve sake without preservatives, it goes through Pasteurisation (this can be done in a tank or in a bottle), where it is heated and cooled multiple times to kill any unwanted bacteria. This process has a dramatic effect on the sake. If we think of sake like garlic, raw it has a powerful strong flavour, but when cooked, it mellows and becomes more nuanced.

Typically sake is pasteurised twice, there are many types of machines and methods that will affect the outcome of the sake.

Maturation

Premium sake is rested for a period to mellow the fresh sakes qualities. However, the brewer may choose to rest it for any amount of time they deem necessary. Most sake will be aged for a short period, typically ranging from 1 to 6 months, but some can be aged for over 20 years. The latter is usually specifically designed for long-term aging purposes.

Adjustment and Bottling
Lastly, sake will need to be diluted before bottling. Some brewers will bottle without dilution, calling it Genshu sake.

Simple Sake Terminology

The below are common terms we might see in the book or on a sake bottle. It's worth noting the Japanese language is extensive and many sake words have secondary meanings or alternative translations. This list is in no way extensive but a good starting point:

Sake (酒): Sake, referred to as Nihonshu (日本酒) in Japan, is a traditional Japanese alcoholic beverage made from rice, water, yeast, and koji mould.

GŌ (合): A unit of measurement, 180ml used in Japan, For example, "ichigō" means one gō, which is 180ml.

Jozo (醸造): Or Jouzou, "fermentery", used specially where the brewery does or did make soy sauce, miso.

Shuzoten (酒造店): Shuzouten, brewery/shop/sales.

Honten (本店): Main branch/office.

Junmai (純米): Junmai means "pure rice" and is a type of sake made only from rice, water, yeast, and koji. It does not contain any added alcohol.

Honjozo (本醸造): Honjozo is a type of sake where a small amount of distilled alcohol is added during brewing. It has a lighter and crisper taste compared to Junmai sake. Honjozo is a premium sake brewed with rice that has been polished to 70% or above of its original size.

Ginjo (吟醸): Ginjo refers to premium sake brewed with rice that has been polished to 60% or above of its original size. It typically undergoes a slower fermentation process at lower temperatures, resulting in a more complex and aromatic flavour profile.

Daiginjo (大吟醸): Daiginjo is the highest grade of sake, brewed with rice that has been polished to at least 50% of its original size. It requires highly skilled craftsmanship and is known for its delicate, refined, fruity and floral flavours.

Nigori (濁り): Nigori sake is cloudy, coarsely filtered sake that still contains rice sediment, giving it a milky appearance. It can be sweeter and has a richer mouthfeel compared to clear sake.

Genshu (原酒): Genshu refers to undiluted sake, meaning it has not been mixed with water after fermentation. As a result, it sometimes has a higher alcohol content and a robust flavour.

Tokubetsu (特別): Special designation normally indicating the use of premium ingredients or production methods.

Futsushu (普通): Ordinary sake with no special designation. Typically had a high percentage of distilled alcohol added and it is consumed in casual settings

Sake Grading and Classification

The Japanese government has implemented various systems and classifications to ensure the quality and authenticity of Japanese Sake over the years.

The current classification system for sake is the "Special Designation of Sake" or Tokutei Meisho-shu (特定名称酒) in Japanese, which categorises sake into specific grades based on the production process and ingredients used. As I discuss the grades in the section, I will focus on a few key points that differentiate each grade but will not be covering all aspect of the Tokutei Meisho-shu system.

The categories include:
Junmai
Honjozo
Junmai Ginjo
Ginjo
Jumai Daiginjo
Daiginjo

And also includes Tokubetsu Junmai and Tokubetsu Honjozo.

The Tokutei Meisho-shu system covers grading but doesn't include "styles" such as cloudy, starting methods, or additional production techniques like aging or carbonation. Meaning you can have all styles of sake with any grading. For instance, Nigori is a type of sake where some of the sake lees have been left in the bottle. It comes in variations like Junmai Nigori and Ginjo Nigori. These styles can also overlap; for example,

Junmai Nigori Awa (Junmai, Cloudy, and sparkling Sake). Understanding these terms is crucial to identifying what is in the bottle.

In this book, when I mention a grade from the Tokutei Meisho-Shu system, unless otherwise stated, it will be a typical sake (no additional styles). If the sake does have another characteristic worth discussing, I will mention this. After covering the Tokutei Meisho-Shu terms, I will discuss relevant styles for mixing, such as Nigori or Aged, etc, and will highlight the sake's grading of any sake mentioned at the same time.

Rice Polishing

When talking about sake, rice polishing will always be mentioned, the rice polishing rate, refers to the percentage of the rice grain remaining after the outer layers have been removed through the polishing process. In the context of sake brewing, this process is crucial as it significantly impacts the final flavour of sake.

The rice polishing rate plays a crucial role in sake brewing because the outer layers of the rice grain contain proteins, fats, and minerals, which will influence the taste of sake. By removing these through polishing, the brewer can access the pure starch core of the rice grain, which is essential for creating a clean, refined, and delicate sake.

Lower Polishing Rate (e.g., 70% or less): Sakes made from rice with a lower polishing rate tend to have a higher concentration of proteins, fats, and minerals. As a result, they might have a richer, fuller, and sometimes robust flavour.

Higher Polishing Rate (e.g., 60% or more): Sakes made from rice with a higher polishing rate have had more of these outer layers removed, leaving mainly the starchy core. This results in a lighter, more refined, and delicate sake. These sakes are often fragrant, and more fruitier.

It's important to note that while the polishing rate is a critical factor, the overall quality of sake is influenced by various other factors, including the quality of rice, water, yeast, and brewing techniques.
The rice polishing rate is usually expressed as a percentage, indicating how much of the grain remains after the process. For example, if a sake label says "60% polishing," it means that 40% of the outer layer has been polished away, leaving 60% of the grain intact.

The Tokutei Meisho-Shu grading falls in line with polishing rates. I will explain each polishing rate in each grades introduction but for reference they are below:

RICE MILLING PERCENTAGE		ALCOHOL– ADDED RICE, WATER, YEAST, KOJI, DISTILLED ALCOHOL	PURE RICE STYLE RICE, WATER, YEAST, KOJI
	50%OR LESS REMAINING	DAIGINJO	JUNMAI DAIGINJO
	60%OR LESS REMAINING	GINJO	JUNMAI GINJO
	70%OR LESS REMAINING	HONJOZO	JUNMAI
	NO MINIMUM MILLING REQUIREMENT	FUTSU–SHU	

Junami	No minimum
Honjozo	70% minimum
Junmai Ginjo/Ginjo	60% minimum
Junmai Daiginjo/Daiginjo	50% minimum

It's important to remember these are minimum, if you exceed these you are able to call your sake whatever you'd like below where it qualifies, for example, if you made a sake to Daiginjo levels, you would be allowed to label it as a Ginjo or Honjozo.

Why would you do this? Typically if this is done it's because the flavour of the sake fits more inline with a lower grading so you'd label it as a lower grade to meet your customers expectations.

Junmai Vs Non-Junmai Sake

Junmai means "pure rice" and is a type of sake made only from rice, water, yeast, and koji. It does not contain any added alcohol. While the word we use here is Pure, this is in the sense it is "untouched", the actually quality of the sake is determined by the end consumer.

Non-Junmai sake, also known as "Alcohol-added sake," or colloquially also known as "Artuen", does include a small amount of distilled alcohol during the brewing process.

The added alcohol is typically called brewers alcohol, (this is most commonly a flavourless high strength spirit imported from Brazil) but this can also be Shochu or other alcohol from agricultural sources.

The addition of alcohol can have several effects on the final product:

Adjusting flavour and aroma: Adding alcohol can help draw out more flavour and aroma from the rice, making the sake, fruitier, or more aromatic.

Increasing yield: Alcohol can increase the overall yield of sake from a given amount of rice, making the production more cost-effective.

Changing texture: Non-Junmai sake may have a lighter body compared to Junmai sake.

Nihonshudo (日本酒度)

Nihonshudo, or Sake Meter Value (SMV), is a scale used to measure the sweetness or dryness of sake. A positive value indicates a drier taste, while a negative value signifies a sweeter taste.

Here's a more detailed description of the Sake Meter Value:

The SMV is a brewing tool used by brewers to track production and constancy, it is determined by measuring the specific gravity of sake relative to the density of water.

The SMV scale ranges from positive to negative numbers:

Positive SMV (+): Sake with a positive value on the SMV scale is considered "dry." This means that the specific gravity of the sake is lower than that of water, indicating that it has a lighter texture and a less sweet taste. Remember *"Higher is drier"*

Negative SMV (-): Sake with a negative value on the SMV scale is considered "sweet." This means that the specific gravity of the sake is higher than that of water, indicating a denser texture and a sweeter taste.

The SMV scale typically ranges from around -15 (very sweet) to +15 (very dry). However, most sake falls within the range of -3 to +5 on the SMV scale, with a slightly dry to slightly sweet taste. This doesn't mean a sake can't be -48, but this is rare.

In addition to the Sake Meter Value (SMV), two other important scales used to describe the characteristics of sake are the Amino Acid Content (Amino) and Acidity scales. These measurements provide further insights into the taste and quality of sake.

Amino Acid Content (Amino)

Often referred to as "Amino," measures the concentration of amino acids present in sake. Amino acids are essential components that contribute to the overall flavour and aroma of sake. Higher levels of amino acids generally result in a rich, full-bodied, and umami-driven sake, while lower levels lead to a lighter and more delicate sake.

Low Amino Content: Sake with lower amino acid levels tends to have a clean, light, and crisp taste.

High Amino Content: Sake with higher amino acid levels will have a more pronounced umami flavour, often described as richer. It may exhibit deeper, complex flavours with a longer finish.

Acidity Content

Or "San-do," measures the acidity level in sake. It indicates the concentration of organic acids, such as lactic acid and succinic acid, which contribute to the overall balance and freshness of the sake's taste.

Low Acidity: Sake with lower acidity tends to be mellow and smooth on the palate. It may have a slightly sweeter perception due to the reduced acidic bite.

High Acidity: Sake with higher acidity will have a more vibrant and lively taste, with a noticeable crispness and a clean finish. It enhances the perception of dryness, even if the sake has residual sweetness.

Both these scales typically range from 1.00 to 2.00.

Combining the information from the Sake Meter Value (SMV), Amino Acid Content (Amino), and Acidity (San-do) scales, you can gain a more comprehensive understanding of a sake's profile:

Dry Sake: A sake with positive SMV, lower Amino content, and higher acidity will have a dry profile with a clean and refreshing finish.

Sweet Sake: A sake with negative SMV, higher Amino content, and lower acidity will have a sweeter taste profile, with a round and smooth mouthfeel.

Umami-driven Sake: A sake with higher Amino content, regardless of the SMV or acidity, will likely showcase pronounced umami flavours and a rich mouthfeel.

Remember that these scales are not isolated indicators but are interconnected elements that, along with other factors like rice polishing ratio, yeast strains, and water hardness, contribute to the overall taste and character of the sake. Exploring different sake varieties with varying values on these scales can be an enjoyable way to discover the diverse and nuanced world of sake flavours.

Sake Drinking Vessels

Sake vessels have been around for as long as sake itself, and they are still evolving today. Below, I've written a brief description of the common drinking vessels. However, it is worth noting that sake vessels are still evolving, and more recently, glassware specific to styles like Daiginjo and Awe has been developed. The main takeaway is to drink from what you enjoy. When I'm drinking alone, a simple white wine glass is my preferred choice, but with friends, I opt for the theatrics of a traditional vessel. Drink from what you enjoy!

Pouring Vessels

Katakuchi: A spouted pitcher/bowl style sake vessel, often made of ceramic or tin, used to pour sake into cups.

Tokkuri: A small ceramic flask used to serve and pour sake. It typically has a narrow neck and a round body.

Drinking Vessels

Ochoko: Small ceramic or glass cups, often cylindrical in shape, used for casual drinking and toasting. They come in various designs and sizes.

Sakazuki: A wide, flat saucer-like cup these are typically designed to hold about about 18ml of sake.

Guinomi: Larger than ochoko, but very similar in all other ways.

Sori Yanagi Sake Glass: Designed by Sori Yanagi, these sake glasses have an lovely upside-down bell shape. Designed for simplicity and practicality while enjoying your sake cold.

Kiriko Glass: The Kiriko glass can take on various shapes and sizes, but it generally boasts a rounded bowl that tapers slightly towards the mouth to concentrate the sake's aromatic profile. Its base may be solid or decorated, with some variations featuring a textured surface to enhance grip and visual appeal.

Kikichoko: A Kikichoko is a small, cylindrical ceramic or glass vessel. The unique feature of the Kikichoko is the blue rings that encircle the inside of the cup. These rings serve as visual indicators, helping the tasters gauge the clarity and colour of the sake, which are essential factors in assessing its quality.

Masu: A square wooden box traditionally used for measuring rice, but now is sometimes employed as a drinking vessel. Made from unfinished cedar wood or lacquer.

Sake Drinking Culture in Japan

Sake holds a significant cultural importance in Japan and is deeply rooted in its history. The way sake is consumed and the etiquette surrounding it play an essential role in Japanese social gatherings and rituals. Here are some key aspects of sake drinking culture in Japan.

Rituals and Traditions: Sake is often involved in various ceremonies and rituals, such as Shinto festivals, weddings, and funerals. It is customary to offer sake to deities, ancestors, or even business partners as a sign of respect and goodwill.

Pouring Etiquette: In a group setting, it is customary for someone else to pour sake for you, and likewise, you pour for others. This mutual pouring shows camaraderie and fosters a sense of bonding among participants. It's worth noting that at some point in the evening, it's acceptable to start pouring your own sake to control your alcohol consumption.

Kanpai (乾杯): Kanpai is a popular Japanese toast used when drinking sake or other alcoholic beverages. It translates to "Cheers!" or "To your health!" and is accompanied by raising your glass and clinking them with others before taking a sip.

Sake and Food Pairings: Sake is often paired with traditional Japanese dishes, enhancing the flavours of the food and the drink. Different sakes complement various types of cuisine, and the pairing can be a culinary adventure.

Junmai

Junmai (純米)

Junmai means "pure rice" and is a type of sake made only from rice, water, yeast, and koji. It does not contain any added alcohol.

It holds a significant place in the world of sake production, known for its historical brewing process (while added alcohol sake is an old style, Junmai predates it).

Unlike other types of sake that may contain additives such as distilled alcohol, Junmai sake is crafted using only four essential ingredients: rice, water, yeast, and koji mould.

This adherence to simplicity makes Junmai sake highly regarded among sake enthusiasts and connoisseurs.

To qualify as Junmai sake, it must meet the following criteria:

Rice Polishing: Junmai is the only category in the Tokutei Meisho-shu system which doesn't have a minimum polishing rate.

No additives: Junmai sake does not contain any additives or enhancers, maintaining the integrity of its natural flavours and characteristics.

Ingredients: Junmai sake is made with only four ingredients - rice, water, yeast, and koji mould. No additional distilled alcohol is added during the brewing process.

Junmai sake is often characterised by its full-bodied and robust nature. The absence of added alcohol allows the natural flavours of the rice and brewing process to shine, resulting in a sake with a rich, umami-driven taste. While sweetness levels can vary among Junmai sake, they typically lean towards being slightly sweeter.

As there is no minimum polishing rate on Junmai it is normally price-conscious in nature, making it a preferred choice for consumers and bartenders. Due to its distinct flavour, most customers will easily identify the cocktail with the unique taste of sake. Junmai sake's rich and full-bodied characteristics contribute a new dimension to a cocktail, making it both approachable and exciting for adventurous drinkers. With its versatility and the ability to complement various ingredients and spirits, Junmai sake opens up a world of creative possibilities in the realm of sake cocktails and a great option if you are trying to explore the fusion of traditional Japanese sake with contemporary mixology.

A Great Example

Brewery: Takasago Shuzo
Prefecture: Hokkaido
Bottle Name: Kokushi Muso Cocoo Junmai
Style: Junmai
Rice: Hokkaido Ginpu
Polishing: 60%

Takasago Shuzo, nestled in the heart of Hokkaido Island in northern Japan, is the artisanal brewery only making Tokutei Meisho-shu sake. Takasago Shuzo takes pride in crafting pure and fresh sake inspired by Hokkaido's signature snowy landscapes. The region's harsh winter climate provides a remarkable advantage, allowing for the implementation of an atypical filtration method, where sake is meticulously filtered under ice domes reconstructed each winter, they then blend this sake with pristine snowmelt water. Both these unique factors contribute to the breweries exceptional quality sakes. Perfectly suited for savouring when chilled, Kokushi Muso Cocoo Junmai is a delicate and harmonious sake, with notes of peach, apricot, apple, pear and of course all while still being an umami rich Junmai.

Saketini 2.0
Created by Gento Torigata

180g	Sake Puree
200ml	Poire Williams (Eau de vie)
100ml	Christian Drouin Calvados
200ml	Fuji Apple Juice
50ml	Sugar syrup
50g	Mascarpone
25ml	Malic Acid solution 6%
5ml	Cardamon Bitters

Glass:	Rocks
Method:	Stir 70ml of the premix over ice
Ice:	Cubed/Block
Garnish:	Sansho Pepper Leaf

Comments:
Combine all ingredients together in a jug and mix properly. A great premix to be kept in the fridge and finished to order or with friends at home!

Sake Purée Recipe
50g	Sakekasu
200ml	Yoshinogawa Junmai

About this sake:
Brewed by Yoshi No Gawa in Niigata prefecture created specifically with a respect for pairing sake with good food, this versatile sake has been crafted with 100% Niigata rice. The lower alcohol content (12%) leaves it with a moderate sweetness, refreshing acidity.

Kaoru Lavander
Created by Maria Victoria Vecchione

30ml	Elderflower St Germain
25ml	Gekkeikan Kome To Mizu Junmai
25ml	Jinzu Gin
5	Limes
3 Disk	Cucumber
1	Teaspoon of brown sugar
A pinch	Dry lavender

Glass:	Julep Glass
Method:	Churned
Ice:	Crushed ice
Garnish:	Shiso leaf

Comments:
Muddle the cucumber with the lime and the brown sugar. Add the lavender, Sake, Gin and St Germain, fill glass with crushed ice to the top. Mix well with the Bar spoon.

About this Sake
This versatile sake is perfect for newcomers. Made from high-quality koshihikari rice, it boasts a delightful dryness complemented by a rich, full-bodied flavour profile. With its fruity aroma and savoury aftertaste.

Royal Kauri Sake Martini
Created by Maria Victoria Vecchione & Mykolas Karanauskas

15ml	Roku Gin
40ml	Gekkeikan Kome To Mizu Junmai
10ml	St Germain
15ml	Cucumber and Martini Bianco cordial
20ml	Lime Cordial

Glass:	Chilled Coup Glass
Method:	Shake & Strain
Ice:	None
Garnish:	Cucumber and Lime Wheel

Comments:
This drink was made to celebrate the coronation of Charles III and his wife, Camilla, as king and queen of the United Kingdom and the other Commonwealth realms, took place on Saturday, 6 May 2023 at Westminster Abbey

Notes:
Cucumber-Vermouth cordial

300ml	Water
100ml	Martini Bianco
100g	Caster Sugar
1	Cucumber
2g	Citric Acid
2g	Malic Acid

Peel the cucumber and soak the cucumber peels in 300 ml of cold water for 10-20 minutes to make a cucumber water. Meanwhile cut the cucumber into small pieces and combine them in a blender with sugar, acids and vermouth. Remove and discard the peels from water. Add the cucumber water to the blender and process until the sugar has dissolved and the cucumber turned into puree. Strain out the solids through the cheesecloth.

Refrigerate in the sealed container for up to one week.

Lime cordial

350ml	Water
250g	Caster Sugar
4g	Citric Acid
2g	Malic Acid
3	Limes (1 peeled, all 3 juiced).

Cut the peel of one lime into thin strips and put them in a jar (or any other airtight container) together with acids and sugar. Close the lid, shake well until combined and leave it for 1 to 2 hours at room temperature. Add all the content of the jar to the blender together with water and juice of 3 limes and blend until smooth. Filter through the fine mesh strainer.

Refrigerate in the sealed container for up to one week.

About this Sake

This versatile sake is perfect for newcomers. Made from high-quality koshihikari rice, it boasts a delightful dryness complemented by a rich, full-bodied flavour profile. With its fruity aroma and savoury aftertaste.

Three Rice Martini
Created by Carlos Perez Bayona

35ml	Toyonaga Kome Shochu
15ml	Awamori
10ml	Rice Vodka
10ml	Tio Pepe
5ml	Italicus

Glass:	Nick & Nora
Method:	Stirred
Ice:	None
Garnish:	Lemon Coin

Comments:
This drink is from the menu of the Shochu Lounge, London 2023.

About this Sake
Toyonaga Kome Shochu is a classic rice shochu from the Kyushu heartland. Exceptionally smooth and mellow, Toyonaga has a sweet meadowland flavour, reminiscent of single malts.

Honjozo

Honjozo (本醸造)
"Honjozo" stands as the initial category of alcohol-added sake in the Tokutei Meisho-Shu system with a minimum of 70% polishing rate. It commonly employs a modest quantity of distilled alcohol, though in more restrained measures compared to what's found in Futsushu.

This style of alcohol-added sake gained prominence in the aftermath of the Second World War. During the war, in an attempt to safeguard rice yields, the Japanese government made it mandatory for sake brewers to incorporate up to 50% imported distilled alcohol into their sake production. This resulted in a significantly drier and more alcoholic profile for the sake (which also happened to be more cost-effective to produce). Following the war, this drier style continued to be popular with the Japanese people.

The deliberate inclusion of a precisely measured amount of added alcohol contributes to a refined and lighter sake profile.

In Japan, the sales of Honjozo have experienced a year-on-year decline. However, from my vantage point as a UK resident, this style is currently experiencing a surge in popularity here. This trend can be largely attributed to the UK's most renowned sake brand launching their lineup with a Honjozo offering.

Honjozo sake frequently provides a more accessible price point while upholding a superior quality in comparison to Futsushu. The drier and lighter flavours, which are its hallmark, make it an excellent choice for cocktail mixing, allowing sake to still shine with other ingredients rather than overpowering or diminishing under them. The presence of a "boozier" taste also aids in distinguishing the sake amidst the diverse components within a cocktail.

A Great Example

Brewery: Akashi-Tai
Prefecture: Hyogo
Bottle Name: N/A
Style: Honjozo Genshu Tokubetsu
Rice: Goyakumangoku
Polishing: 60%

The Akashi-Tai Brewery, situated in the harbour town of Akashi in southwestern Japan, draws its name from this area and "Tai," which means fish. As sea bream can be seen challenging waters along Akashi's shoreline.

For over a century and a half, this family-operated brewery has stood against the relentless tides of time, tracing back its origins to 1856. Rooted in the essence of familial unity, they remain steadfast in their dedication to crafting extraordinary sakes using locally sourced ingredients.
Guided by the expertise passed down through multiple generations, every Akashi-Tai sake embodies the enduring passion that the Yonezawa family holds for their craft, now under the stewardship of Toji, Kimio Yonezawa.

This sake is a lavish and undiluted creation, fashioned from Gohyakumangoku rice that has been polished to 60% of its original size. While Honjozo specifications require a minimum of 70% polishing, the brewery has opted to surpass this threshold in pursuit of the specific qualities they seek. The outcome is a more substantial iteration of their honjozo tokubetsu variety, boasting intensified fruity notes and a weightier mouthfeel.

Jasminum
Created by Klára Kopčiková

20ml	Shirayuki Itami Morohaku Honjozo
20ml	Cucumber infused El Tequileño Tequila
15ml	Gabriel Boudier peach
50ml	Cold Brew jasmine tea
10ml	2:1 Sugar Syrup
3 Dash	20% Saline solution
2 Dash	Bitter Truth celery bitters

Glass:	Rocks
Method:	Stirred
Ice:	Cubed
Garnish:	Red amaranth

Comments:
A light cocktail, the sake adds an umami quality to the cucumber and tequila. Great for drinking in the summer at a BBQ! This drink was created for the 2022 Winter menu of The Pineapple Club, the UK's 14th Best Bar (Top 50 Cocktails Bars 2023).

Cucumber El Tequileño
300g	Cucumber
1000ml	El Tequileño Tequila

Chop the cucumber into quarters and add to tequila. Leave for 6 hours and strain out the solids.

About this sake

The Morohaku technique, utilising polished rice for both koji and kake-mai, was originated during the Muromachi Period and gained prominence in the 17th century with the Itami Morohaku style of sake from Hyogo Prefecture, known for its low acidity and clear appearance. This style's rise was aided by Nada's water-driven polishing capabilities.

The Itami Morohaku sake offers aromas of banana, red apple, bread, and sweet yogurt, accompanied by stewed plum and pineapple. Its medium-bodied, round, buttery texture is enhanced when warmed.

The Shirayuki Itami Morohaku Honjozo won an IWC Trophy in 2020.

Bonsai
Created by Alexander Taylor

60ml	Akashi-Tai Honjozo Tokubetsu
7.5ml	Drouin Blanche Calvados
7.5ml	Giffard Lychee
50ml	Rich "textured" Syrup
1 Dash	Yuzu bitters

Glass:	Pony
Method:	Stirred
Ice:	None
Garnish:	None

Comments:
A sake forward take on the classic bamboo cocktail made by Alexander Taylor for Koi in Cardiff, UK. As he put it "This is an absolute slapper of a 'tini"

Rich "textured" Syrup
2:1 Simple Syrup, douse in lactic acid and salt to taste.

About this sake:
This Tokubetsu Honjozo is crafted using Gohyakumangoku rice from Hyogo Prefecture, with a rice polishing ratio of 60%. This rice, along with the Honjozo style, gives it its lighter body and pleasant savouriness. It offers a longer, more robust finish and boasts a delicate bouquet and subtle hints of lemon, lime, and straw. The recommended serving temperature ranges from 6 to 50°C, allowing for versatility in its enjoyment.

Cheap Vacation
Created by Alexander Taylor

20ml	Koskenkorva Vodka
30ml	Akashi-Tai Honjozo Tokubetsu
10ml	Coconut-Muyu jasmine
20ml	Lactic kiwi syrup
30ml	Coconut milk
1 Drop	Absinthe

Glass:	Hurricane
Method:	Shaken and Strained
Ice:	Crushed
Garnish:	Kiwi slice and Cocktail umbrella

Comments:
For this drink, Alex wanted to accentuate the savoury, banana-like notes of Tokubetsu sake. The combination of lactic kiwi and coconut gives it a similarity to a Calpico ice lolly, and the overall makes it taste incredibly escapist, hence the name.

Lactic kiwi

20g	Lactic Acid
2g	Salt
1000ml	Giffard Kiwi Syrup

Add all ingredients together and mix until solids are dissolved.

Coconut Muyu
Add 50% melted coconut oil by weight to Muyu Jasmine Verte Liqueur for 2 hour. Refrigerate mixture and and filter liquid

away from solids

About this sake:
This Tokubetsu Honjozo is crafted using Gohyakumangoku rice from Hyogo Prefecture, with a rice polishing ratio of 60%. This rice, along with the Honjozo style, gives it its lighter body and pleasant savouriness. It offers a longer, more robust finish and boasts a delicate bouquet and subtle hints of lemon, lime, and straw. The recommended serving temperature ranges from 6 to 50°C, allowing for versatility in its enjoyment.

Yon
Created by Matteo basso

70ml	Akashi-Tai Honjozo Genshu Tokubetsu
10ml	Akashi-Tai umeshu
5ml	Sugar syrup (1:1)
3 Dash	Teapot bitter

Glass:	Rocks
Method:	Build
Ice:	Cubed
Garnish:	Discarded grapefruit peel & pandan leaf

Comments:
Yon is the Japanese word for four, a Old fashioned style of cocktail based on four element, in order to elevate the sake and make it protagonist of the drink.
This drink was the Winner of the UKBG National Akashi-Tai cocktail competition 2021

About this sake:
Fuller in body and with a higher alcohol content, this Tokubetsu Honjozo Genshu offers more concentrated flavour than the standard Akashi-Tai Tokubetsu Honjozo.

Ginjo Style Sake

Ginjo (吟醸) Meaning meticulous fermentation/manufacturing.

Daiginjo (大吟醸) Meaning big meticulous fermentation/ manufacturing.

The term "Ginjo" is often used to encompass all styles within this category, including Ginjo, Junmai Ginjo, Daiginjo, and Junmai Daiginjo. These are regarded as the pinnacle of sake craftsmanship. Ginjo sakes require a minimum polishing rate of 60% under the Tokutei Meisho-Shu System, while Daiginjo, being even more refined, is a minimum polishing rate of 50%. The words Ginjo and Daiginjo are synonymous with exceptional quality and demanding production processes.

For Ginjo to come to fruition as we know it today, a few things were needed: new techniques and new technology. Ginjo techniques or soft water techniques were developed around 1887 by Mr. Senzaburou Miura. Miura found himself in Hiroshima, a region initially considered unsuitable for sake production due to its soft spring water. Miura had travelled Japan and studied sake production in Nada, where the sake industry had flourished for centuries thanks to its hard water, ideal for brewing sake. Hiroshima's soft water lacked the minerals necessary to nourish starter cultures crucial for brewing. Around 1887, Miura pioneered a new soft water brewing method, helping to give birth to the "Ginjo" style. Faced with the challenges of Hiroshima's soft water, he meticulously experimented with temperature and humidity controls, perfecting a refined brewing method by 1898.

Ginjo style sake technology started to emerge in 1933 with the invention of the vertical rice-polishing machine. This revolutionised rice milling, an integral step in the process. With the joint efforts of breweries, advancements in refrigeration technology, and the discovery of new yeast strains, the quality of Ginjo sake improved significantly in a short span.

This improvement set the stage for a Ginjo sake boom in the early 1980s, leading to the rapid growth of this premium sake category in both Japan and worldwide.

Dewazakura brewery became the first brewery in Japan to make Ginjo sake accessible to the general public through their release of Cherry Bouquet "Oka" Ginjo.

Ginjo Sake is renowned for its clean, crisp, and fruity flavour profile, often boasting notes of apple, pear, melon, and delicate floral undertones. Its aroma is both fragrant and aromatic.

Daiginjo Sake offers a similarly clean and delicate profile, enriched with intricate fruity, floral, and sometimes herbal notes. Its aroma is fragrant and brimming with a medley of fruits.

While Ginjo and Daiginjo sakes are traditionally enjoyed on their own, they have very unique characteristics when it comes to mixing. Their clean and crisp profiles, coupled with fruity and floral notes, make them excellent ingredients. However, these styles can be easily be overpowered by other flavours. Much to my frustration, this often leads to a waste of great sake and a lacklustre drink. My advice when using these styles is to treat the sake as a base and build around its unique profile. Use fewer additional ingredients and allow the sake to be the main event!

A Great Example

Brewery: Miyasaka Brewing Company
Prefecture: Nagano
Bottle Name: Masumi Nanago
Style: Junmai Daiginjo Yamahai
Rice: Kinmonnishiki
Polishing: 40%

Masumi stands as a revered name in the world of sake, earning admiration across Japan (and the world) for its delightful flavour and unwavering commitment to dependable craftsmanship. The brewery responsible for its creation dates back to 1662 in the town of Suwa, a place renowned for its precision in silk spinning. Today, meticulous attention to detail remains the cornerstone of Masumi's brewing philosophy.

In 1921, the brewery's president, Masaru Miyasaka, selected a 28-year-old sake prodigy named Chisato Kubota to be the brewmaster. Together, they embarked on a journey akin to Zen monks, seeking wisdom by visiting seasoned masters. This profound dedication to enhancing the quality of Masumi sake, coupled with an open-minded approach, bore fruit in 1943 when Miyasaka Brewing Company earned its initial prestigious accolade at the Japan National Sake Appraisal.

Masumi's reputation soared even higher in 1946, when their entries claimed the first, second, and third positions in the competition. This astonishing achievement piqued the curiosity of an expert from the National Research Institute of Brewing, who requested samples of their unfiltered sake for analysis. His research unveiled the presence of a completely novel yeast strain, subsequently christened Association No. 7.

In the realm of sake, the discovery of a new yeast strain is akin to receiving the Nobel Prize, a distinction enjoyed by a select few breweries. The gentle and pleasing aroma of No. 7, along with its user-friendly nature, quickly took over Nagano Prefecture, and today, it remains the choice of over half of Japan's breweries.

In 2002, when the brewery introduced its first Yamahai Junmai Daiginjo sake, they christened it "Nanago" (No. 7) in homage to the remarkable microorganism that has left an indelible mark on the brewing world.

Rice
Created by Klára Kopčiková

75ml	Konishi Shuzo Daiginjo Hiyashibori
25ml	Gabriel Boudier crème de cacao blanc
10ml	Homemade 1:1 vinilla syrup

Glass:	Rocks
Method:	Stirred
Ice:	Block
Garnish:	White chocolate button

Comments:
This beverage beautifully demonstrates the versatility of sake. While vanilla and butterscotch notes are often associated with sake that has aged beyond its prime, this drink defies that stereotype. It offers a rich and creamy mouthfeel, thanks to the lactic acid naturally found in sake, which complements the creme de cacao and vanilla. The additional alcohol in the sake enhances the esters in both the sake itself and the cocktail, elevating the overall drinking experience.

Homemade 1:1 Vanilla Syrup
Boil a 1:1 Simple syrup and removed from the heat add 1 sliced and deseeded vanilla pod per 2 litres and infused for 3 hours. Strain out any solids with a cheese cloth.

About this sake:
Drawing upon over 450 years of brewing expertise, Konishi employs their 'hiyashibori' pressing technique pressing the Sake at frigid temperatures with minimal exposure to air to prevent oxidation to craft this Daiginjo. On the olfactory front,

it presents a delicate bouquet of fruity notes, featuring hints of citrus, cherry, and pear. This sake is characterised by its light body, cleanliness, elegance, and simplicity, boasting a mild acidity and subtle flavours of citrus, cucumber, and pear.

Konishi Daiginjo Hiyashibori, a consistent recipient of the Grand Gold Medal at the Fine Sake Awards (last awarded in 2021), is the culmination of extensive research and development conducted by Konishi Shuzo's experimental division, which crafts sake under the family's prestigious name.

The Virtuous Cocktail
Created by Stuart Hudson

60ml	Toku Junmai Daiginjo sake
10ml	Umeshu
10ml	Kukicha tea
10ml	Dry vermouth
2 Dash	Tiki bitters

Glass:	Martini
Method:	Stirred
Ice:	None
Garnish:	Ume plum

Comments:
This cocktail was created to showcase Toku Junmai Daiginjo.

About this sake
Toku is a super-premium Junmai Daiginjo sake, crafted in Japan's coldest city, Asahikawa, Hokkaido. Brewed in freezing conditions, it starts with pure water from the Daisetsuzan mountains and highly polished Yamadanishiki rice. The rice is polished to an exceptional 35%, well above the required polishing rate for this style of sake (50%), often considered the highest level attainable while maintaining a reasonable price for consumers. This bottling is also a Namachozo, meaning the sake only undergoes one pasteurisation (heat-treatment). Sake typically undergoes two. This helps keep its original fresh taste. It is best enjoyed chilled at 5°C. Much like fine white wine, it is recommended to use stemware and savour the temperature change from fridge to glass to fully appreciate its Hokkaido heritage and exquisite complexity.

Kuma Gimlet
Created by Glenn Eldridge

40ml	Wandering Poet Junmai Ginjo
20ml	Suntory Roku
10ml	Fino sherry
35ml	Grapefruit cordial
3 dashes	Peach Bitters

Glass:	Rocks
Method:	Stirred
Ice:	Block
Garnish:	White Chocolate Button

Comments:
This is a split base gimlet made for the first menu of ROKA Dubai. The idea was to make a variation of a classic gimlet with the same intensity and clarity of grapefruit flavour but at a slightly more approachable ABV for guests not wanting a drink with the strength of the classic gimlet.

Grapefruit cordial
100g	Grapefruit peels
300g	Caster sugar
600g	Water
Citric acid	
Malic acid	
Tartaric acid	

Method:

Make an oleo under vacuum with the grapefruit peels and sugar and leave at room temperature for 24 hours. After 24 hours add the water to dissolve the sugar. Fine strain to remove the peels. Weigh the yield and acidify by weight with the below ratios.

1.5% Citric
1.5% malic
2% tartaric

About this sake:
Rihaku, a renowned sake brand, takes its name from the illustrious 8th-century Chinese poet, Li Po, who was famed for his poetic prowess and penchant for consuming generous quantities of sake while crafting a hundred poems. This sake originates from the Rihaku Brewing Company, nestled in Shimane, a region characterised by its sparse population and bountiful natural resources.

With a broad appeal and a robust, memorable profile, Rihaku's Junmai Ginjo stands out as a versatile choice, capable of harmonising with even the most challenging of food. Crafted using the prized Yamadanishiki rice, widely acclaimed as the epitome of sake rice quality, this sake showcases a remarkable richness and dryness that captivates the palate.

Futsushu

Futsushu (普通酒)

Futsushu, often referred to as "table sake," is a type of sake that stands apart from all we've discussed so far. There are a few reasons the sake you have might be a Futsushu. Typically, the sake has a large amount of distilled alcohol added (far greater than the amount used in non-Junmai Tokutei Meisho-Shu sake). The other reason could be down to the quality of the ingredients. If the rice didn't hit the shuzo kotekimai (premium sake rice) standards required to make Tokutei Meisho-Shu, for example, the resulting sake would be a Futsushu regardless of the rest of the brewing process.

While Futsushu may not adhere to the same strict standards as sake in the Tokutei Meisho-Shu system, it holds its own significance in the world of sake production. The inclusion of added alcohol can result in a much lighter style of sake, while the typical lower polishing rate, retains a lot of amino acids.

While in the western world, Futsushu normally has a bad reputation, which isn't always warranted, Futsu can be great sake when made well.

Futsushu sake often comes at a more affordable price point than premium sake. This affordability makes Futsushu a popular choice for various settings, including restaurants and casual gatherings in Japan, however it is less common among menus in the western world (outside of cheap sushi bars…).

It's lighter profile and approachable characteristics can also make it a suitable choice for mixing in cocktails. Its affordability and adaptability are great for creative experimentation in the world of mixology.

A Great Example

Brewery: Tsuji Honten
Prefecture: Okayama
Bottle Name: Gozenshu Tougai Omachi 50
Style: Futsu-shu Bodaimoto Muroka Nama Genshu
Rice: Tougai Omachi
Polishing: 50%

Tsuji Honten based in Okayama prefecture, is ran by a dynamic duo consisting of the President and a Master Brewer (Toji), who also happen to be siblings, together they are upholding their family's time-honoured traditions. They stand at the forefront of innovation, masterfully brewing with Omachi rice and the ancient bodaimoto brewing method to craft sake with deep, rustic flavours. Their moto being "The Future of Omachi is Gozenshu."

Gozenshu Tougai Omachi 50 exemplifies the Japanese principle of Mottainai or 'no waste.' It's a namazake (unpasteurised sake) released seasonally in December in Japan. It offers a balanced, fresh, juicy, and rounded profile with lively acidity.

Tsuji Honten, along with other Okayama breweries, collaborates with local farmers in the "Tokujo Omachi Project" to cultivate top-quality Omachi Rice. Though the project yields superb rice, not all meets the requirements for Shuzo Kotekimai (premium sake rice). Rice that falls short of these standards due to flaws is termed Tougai-Mai and can't be used for premium sake. However, some brewers recognise the value in using Tougai-Mai, producing remarkable Futsushu sakes.

Gozenshu Tougai Omachi 50 boasts a gentle aroma of sour plum, green banana, rhubarb, custard, strawberry, and lemon sherbet, with hints of herbs and nuts. It has a medium body, plump, juicy texture, and a rustic vibe, complemented by mouthwatering acidity that ties everything together.

Side note:
Japanese sake brewing has historically been and continues to be a predominantly male-dominated field. Maiko Tsuji, the seventh-generation brewer of Tsuji Honten, is among the few female Toji in Japan. While I'm uncertain of the exact number of female Toji currently in Japan, it's believed to be under 50, which amounts to approximately 3% or less of breweries operated by women.

Tamagozake
Created by Klára Kopčiková and Samuel Boulton

30ml	Gozenshu Futsushu
10ml	VS Brandy
10ml	Cinnamon Shochu
75ml	Egg Nog

Glass:	Coup
Method:	Shake & Fine Strain
Ice:	None
Garnish:	Grated Nutmeg

Comments:
An innovative twist on the classic Japanese beverage, Tamagozake. This is a contemporary rendition of the traditional which incorporates sake, egg, and a touch of natural sweetness, often from honey.

Egg Nog Recipe - 50 Serves

3000ml	Whole milk
1000ml	Double cream
800g	Egg yolks
800g	Sugar
2.5g	Ground clove
5g	Ground nutmeg
7.5g	Almond Essence

Mix all ingredients together in a pan, and heat gentle so not to cook the egg yolks, this can also be cooked sous vide.

About this sake:
While futsushu may not hold the prestigious title of 'special designation sake,' it possesses a wealth of merits that should not be underestimated. Gozenshu futsushu stands out as a prime example of a futsushu that strikes a delightful balance, offering a palatable experience without the cost. This sake is a delectable and comforting choice, boasting enticing aromas of sweet cereal, soy, and mushrooms with a velvety and creamy rice flavour.

Caffè Corretto
Created by Samuel Boulton

40ml	Meijou Futsushu
20ml	Cafe Borghetti
20ml	Miso Caramel Condensed Milk
1	Egg White

Glass:	Small Rocks
Method:	Shake & Fine Strain
Ice:	None
Garnish:	Grated Nutmeg

Comments:
Similar in richness to a classic flip, but the added miso replaces the yolk.

Miso Caramel Condensed Milk
Remove label from the unopened can of condensed milk. Fill a deep medium saucepan with water. Bring to the boil. Carefully place the can in the saucepan, ensuring there's enough water to completely cover the can at all times, topping up water frequently throughout the cooking process. Simmer, uncovered for 3 hours. Ensure the can is completely covered with water at all times during cooking.

Carefully remove the can from the boiling water. Allow to cool completely before opening.

Decant caramelised condensed milk and add miso paste to your liking and stir until dissolved.

About this sake:
Meijou stands out as an exceptional everyday table sake. It has a well-balanced profile, and remarkable versatility in terms of the range of temperatures at which it can be savoured. Despite being classified as a futsu-shu, Michisakari has exceeded expectations by polishing the rice to 60%.

Sake Wibble
Created by Samuel Boulton

30ml	Kikumasamune Futsushu Gin Pack
25ml	Sloe Gin
25ml	Fresh Grapefruit Juice
5ml	Lemon Juice
5ml	Simple Syrup 2:1
5ml	Creme De Mure

Glass:	Coup
Method:	Shake & Fine Strain
Ice:	None
Garnish:	Lemon Zest

Comments:
A take on the classic Wibble cocktail created by Dick Bradsell in 1999 at The Player in London.

About this sake:
A modern Futsushu from the historical producer Kikumasamune, this Modern Futsu won the Futsu-Shu Trophy at the IWC Great Value Champion Sake 2023 competition. Expect notes of red apple skin, a soft texture, creamy yogurt undertones, a hint of grapefruit zest, melon rind, and a touch of white pepper.

The following styles of sake are not categorised separately by the Tokutei Meishō-shu system, but they are unique sake styles that can be applied alongside the system.

Kimoto/Yamahai

Kimoto (生酛)
Yamahai (山廃)

To grasp the impact of Kimoto and Yamahai on the style and flavour of the sake, we must delve into the technique and historical context of sake production.

In sake making, the terms 'Shubo' or 'Moto' refer to the yeast starter or starter culture. This is where a small portion of the raw ingredients come together to form the foundation, similar to a sour mash in Tennessee whiskey. The purpose of creating the Shubo is to nurture an abundant and healthy yeast population. In modern sake brewing, this is achieved (most commonly) through one of three methods. The most common approach is the 'modern' Sokujo method, while the other two are 'traditional' methods known as Kimoto and Yamahai.

The Kimoto yeast starter method is one of the oldest still in use and was developed during the Edo period. Following this, a slightly newer Yamahai method emerged in the Meiji period. Both of these methods rely on cultivating lactic bacteria, which are present in the environment, to naturally produce lactic acid in the starter. This lactic acid serves as a safeguard against contamination by undesirable microorganisms. In the Sokujo method, lactic acid is simply purchased and added to the raw ingredients, instantly protecting the yeast.

The Kimoto starter culture involves mixing and kneading the starter using poles with blunted blocks attached to the ends.

This process is repeated several times a day for a couple of days. This method yields yeast with a high alcohol tolerance, ensuring active fermentation even as the sake brewing process nears completion. Consequently, this results in a robust, earthy, and sometimes funky brew.

The Yamahai method, in contrast, skips the labor-intensive pole mixing. Instead, the sake is left to ferment without disturbance. Yamahai sake is characterised by its rich texture, elevated levels of umami and acidity, and a touch of sweetness. Notable flavours often include hints of mushrooms or gaminess.

One last starter method to mention is Bodaimoto. While the scope of this book won't cover it, Bodaimoto is one of the oldest starter methods known. If you're interested in learning more, you can listen to the Bodaimoto episode of *Sake Deep Dive* Podcast.

A Great Example

Brewery: Kinoshita Brewing Company
Prefecture: Kyoto - Kinki region
Bottle Name: Tamagawa Red Label
Style: Heirloom Yamahai Junmai Nama Genshu
Rice: Heirloom Kitanishiki
Polishing: 66%

Kinoshita Brewing Company, founded in 1842, is renowned for crafting exceptionally flavourful and refreshing sakes. Notably, since 2008, the brewery has been under the guidance of Philip Harper, who holds the unique title of being the first non-Japanese Toji in all of Japan.

Located just a short five-minute jaunt from the Japan Sea coast in the northern reaches of Kyoto Prefecture, this area has long been celebrated for its rice production. The brewery's advantageous location, blessed with snowy winters and access to pristine spring water from the nearby mountain, provides the ideal conditions for producing exceptional sake.

The Tamagawa Red Label, is crafted with natural yeasts that thrive within the brewery. It's worth noting this sake is incredibly stronger in flavour than typical Yamahai, as it has an impressively high acidity level of 2.9, making it a standout choice for understanding how intense the Yamahai method can be. Red Label is also bottled directly from the press without any filtration, dilution, or other interventions. Its bold and distinctive taste makes it an excellent companion for a wide range of culinary experiences, from hearty stews and grilled meats to delicate oysters and even pungent blue cheeses.

Saikyō
Created by Robert Wood

35ml	Tamagawa Time Machine Junmai Kimoto Sake
35ml	Suntory Chita whisky
6 drops	Mugi bitters
2.5ml	Organic brown rice syrup

Glass:	Kimura Mikumi S4
Method:	Prebatched pour 90ml per serve
Ice:	None
Garnish:	None

Comments: An 1884 Manhattan adaptation named for a previous moniker for Kyoto meaning 'Western Capital'. Lighter than a traditional Manhattan but umami rich and almost fruity with rich cereal qualities.

Mugi Bitters

100ml	Dr. Adam Elmegirab's Teapot bitters
10g	Roasted barley tea (mugicha)

Seal all ingredients in small vac bag and seal. Allow to infuse for 2 hours. Pass through 100u Superbag and store in dasher bottle.

About this sake:
Brewed using a 1712 recipe, "Time Machine" is a delightful and sweet sake with hints of molasses and dried fruit. It captures the essence of sakes from 300 years ago, with abundant umami, natural organic acids, and sugars. Unlike contemporary ginjo styles, this brew has significantly higher levels of acids and amino acids, resulting in a wonderfully sweet taste without being overly sugary.

Aged Sake

Koshu (古酒)

I want to preface this section by mentioning that sake is rarely aged in barrels. Taruzake (more on this later) uses cedar, and some modern sakes are starting to explore use french wine barrels, but typically, an aged sake is stored in an inert vessel, such as stainless steel or clay. However, aging sake for extended periods has been a breakthrough in the sake industry, overturning the conventional idea that sake should be consumed as soon as possible for its best performance. Most sake is designed to be consumed within one year after production, as the aging process is delicate and fraught with complications. Therefore, aged sake is very rare, accounting for less than 1% of all the sake produced in Japan.

To qualify as Koshu (aged sake), the sake must have been aged for more than three years at the brewery. Aged sake is vastly different from any other sake mentioned so far. This aging process can significantly alter the taste and aroma of the sake compared to a freshly brewed batch. Aged sake typically develops a more complex and layered profile, with flavours such as caramel, toffee, nuts, dried fruits, and spices. These flavours are often described as more mature compared to the vibrant and fruity notes of younger sake. Aged sake often exhibits a very pronounced umami quality, reminiscent of savoury, earthy, and even mushroom like flavours. Aging can lead to changes in colour, with some aged sake having a deeper golden or amber hue. The sharpness of alcohol tends to mellow, while sweetness may increase due to water evaporation over time. The exact taste of aged sake can vary widely depending on factors like the quality of the original sake, storage conditions, aging duration, and, of course, the brewery's skill and style, all of which play a significant role.

A Great Example

Brewery: Shiraki Tsunesuke Brewery
Prefecture: Gifu
Bottle Name: Daruma Masamune 5 Year Old
Style: 5 year Old Koshu
Rice: Nipponbare
Polishing: 70%

Shiraki Tsunesuke Brewery, established in 1866, sits proudly by the Nagara River, where they draw pristine water from. To set themselves apart from other sake producers, they took a distinctive turn in the 1960s with the inception of their aged sake line, spearheaded by the Daruma Masamune brand. This remarkable series comprises aged sakes, including 5, 10, and 20-year variants.

Daruma Masamune holds a prominent position in the world of sake, for their rich aged style. They craft sake with elevated levels of umami, amino acids, and sweetness, allowing them to mature gracefully in both bottle and large storage tanks in the brewery's natural ambient temperatures. These temperatures fluctuate, ranging from near freezing in winter to around 26 degrees Celsius in summer. It's these unique conditions that contribute to the lush and unctuous character that Daruma Masamune is renowned for.

The 5-year-old Koshu, boasts a captivating medium amber shade and an enchanting bouquet of dried apricot, bone broth, and honey. The palate revels in a rich umami essence, perfectly balanced with notes of coffee, deep caramel, brazil nut, and dried banana. The texture is delightfully chewy, culminating in a smooth, approachable finish. Remarkably easy to savour.

Sumo
Created by Samuel Boulton

35ml	Michisakari brewery Aperitif koshu
35ml	Imo shochu
25ml	Giffard chocolate cookie syrup
2 Dash	20% Saline

Glass:	Rocks
Method:	Stirred
Ice:	Block
Garnish:	Chocolate cookie

Comments:
This drink is my interpretation of bringing Japanese and Western cultures together. Here you have a Koshu sake providing a rich miso-like Umami back bone to the cocktail, the Imozake (a sweet potato shochu) adding to this, which pairs with the cookie and saline. The drink tastes like a biscuit. Typically, autolytic flavours (that "biscuity breadiness") are often hard to replicate in cocktails, but here you really feel the full cookie flavour.

About this sake
Crafted by Michisakari brewery, renowned since 1771 and situated in Tajima, Gifu this sake was originally brewed in 2008! Made from Miyamanishiki sake rice polished to an impressive Daiginjo level of 40%. With its dark amber hue akin to aged whisky and a rich aroma that boasts notes of walnuts, spices, mushrooms, and malt, Aperitif is sweet (SMV of -32) and offers a complex profile featuring toffee, barley, and nutty nuances. This sake is reminiscent of slightly sweet

sherry, is aptly named for its role as a pre-meal delight, yet it gracefully complements desserts like cheesecake, crumble, and cheese, or serves as a luxurious after-dinner indulgence.

Forest Mist

Created by Roberto Dimitov

50ml	1984 The Bitter Sweet Symphony
25ml	Preserved Honey

Glass:	Kimura Glass
Method:	Stirred
Ice:	Carved Ice Block
Garnish:	Wood Smoke & Fig cracker to cover with green moss, strawberry flowers, edible flowers, glued Isomat bee.

Comments:
This drink was created by Roberto Dimitov for this book.

Preserved Honey

1kg	Figs
500g	Acacia Honey
200g	Golden Berries
4	Fig Leaf
10	Strawberry Leaf
30g	Mountain tea Stalks

About this sake
An aged Kijoshu sake, originally brewed in 1984 and patiently aged until its release in 2016 through a crowdfunding campaign by the brewers. Its profound transformation is evident in its deep, almost obsidian hue, where the trademark sweetness of Kijoshu has gracefully receded. With an aroma reminiscent of fragrant Western-style liqueurs, this sake, christened after The Verve's iconic song "The Bitter Sweet Symphony," captivates the senses with notes of balsamic

vinegar, soy sauce, kombu dashi, and piccalilli. On the first sip, a burst of flavours unfolds, unveiling the complexities of ponzu sauce, Shaoxing wine, umami undertones, and a subtle sweetness similar to caramelised onions.

Sasha, is that you?
Created by Klára Kopčiková

25ml	Daruma Masamune 5 year old
25ml	Chocolate nigori
15ml	Beurre Noisette washed honey syrup
7.5ml	Noix de la Saint Jean
2 Dash	Angostura
5 Dash	20% Saline solution

Glass:	Pony Glass
Method:	Shake & Fine Strain
Ice:	None
Garnish:	Grated Nutmeg

Comments:
This drink was created by Klára Kopčiková for this book.

Beurre Noisette washed honey syrup
70g	Honey
35g	Water
25g	Beurre Noisette

Combine all ingredients and stir, let infuse over night at room temperature, then refrigerate until butter solidifies and strain remaining liquid.

About this sake
Daruma Masamune 5-Year-Old, is a beautiful example of Koshu. While only 5 years old, this sake is complex and thought-provoking!

Nigori

Nigori (濁り)

Literally translating to "cloudy sake,". What sets Nigori apart is the presence of rice solids, (or "lees"), suspended within the liquid. While Nigori is technically considered unfiltered, it's worth noting that all sake legally undergoes some form of filtration. Nigori is made by either gently filtering or pressing the sake, leaving some solids behind, or reintroducing the lees post-production, (the later helps to maintaining consistency for larger brands). This style offers a wide spectrum of textures and sweetness levels.

When opening a new bottle of Nigori, it's likely the lees will have settled at the bottom, I like to syphon off a small clear bit and the top to try next the the rest of the bottle after I have given it a gentle shake to mix in the solids. I probably would not do this when dealing with a sparkling variety!

Nigori is one of the top contenders in mixing, as the lees contribute a slightly creamier texture to the sake, and the varying levels of sweetness help travel sake's profile in mixed drinks. It's essential to remember when mixing with Nigori, you'll always end up with a cloudy cocktail, so be considerate of this, as it will impact the aesthetics of your drink.

A side note, when food pairing Nigori is one of the few sakes great with spicy food!

A Great Example

Brewery: Yamatogawa Shuzo
Prefecture: Fukushima
Bottle Name: Yauemon Tsukiakari Junmai Nigorizake
Style: Junmai Nigori
Rice: Yume no Kaori
Polishing: 65%

Yamatogawa Shuzo, a revered brewery with a 200-year legacy, stands as a bastion of tradition and craft in the world of sake. It has garnered acclaim for its outstanding sake, meticulously produced from organically cultivated rice. Led by President Yauemon Sato, the ninth-generation of family brewery, the focus remains on creating sake that harmonises seamlessly with food. This brewery's hallmark is deep, nuanced flavours that elevate the dining experience. Situated in the northeastern part of Japan, Yamatogawa Shuzo has a storied history dating back to its founding in 1790 during Japan's seclusion under the Tokugawa Shogunate. Today, it proudly maintains over two centuries of tradition while adapting to the times. The brewery's idyllic location in Kitakata, surrounded by nature and renowned for rice cultivation and delectable ramen noodles, adds to its charm. Kitakata's climate, with hot, humid summers and frigid winters, creates ideal conditions for the art of sake brewing.

One of Yamatogawa Shuzo's standout creations is Yauemon Tsukiakari Junmai Nigorizake, a remarkable nigori sake. With its velvety texture, alluring aroma, and impeccably balanced sweetness, it offers a truly captivating experience. This sake is fairly thick and sweet, making it great for pairing with spicy dishes.

Kumori
Created by Thomas Ryan-Tarrant

40ml	Hakutsuru, Junmai Nigori Sayuri
20ml	Amaro Montenegro
20ml	Suze
20ml	Lemon Juice

Glass:	Nick & Nora
Method:	Shake & Strain
Ice:	None
Garnish:	Lemon Twist

Comments:
This delightful cocktail, known as "Kumori," was originally concocted for a special Japanese food market event in Exeter UK. The name "Kumori," which translates to "cloudy" in Japanese. The name was chosen as it mirrors not only the cocktail's soft and inviting pastel colour but also pays homage to the unpredictable weather often experienced in Exeter. This harmonious blend of flavours captures the essence of a serene and cloudy day.

About this sake
Founded in 1743 by Jihei Kano, Hakutsuru initially catered exclusively to their local market for several decades. However, as the years passed, the Hakutsuru brand steadily gained recognition and prestige. Its moment in the global spotlight arrived when it was showcased at the 1900 Paris World Fair. One of their signature offerings, the Hakutsuru Junmai Nigori Sayuri Sake, embodies a light, smooth, and subtly sweet character, owing to its unique coarse filtering process. It is

creamy and light on the palate, with a touch of sweetness and some fruity notes reminiscent of melon, pear, or banana, all underpinned by a gentle rice note.

Koji Colada
Created by Samuel Boulton

70ml	Yauemon Junmai Nigori
70ml	Fresh Blended Pineapple Juice
20ml	Coco Real

Glass:	Highball
Method:	Shake & Strain
Ice:	Cubed
Garnish:	Pineapple Leaves

Comments:
This cocktail relies on freshly blended and strained pineapple juice, as it requires the high acidity level for optimal freshness.

About this sake
Yauemon Sato, the President of Yamatogawa Shuzo, continues the ancestral tradition of crafting sake that enhances dining experiences. Yauemon Junmai Nigori is a sweet nigori sake, embodying this philosophy. Coarsely filtered to retain rice lees, it offers a rich mouthfeel, a fragrant aroma, and a sweet rice flavour. The rice used is homegrown Fukushima rice, Yume no Kaori. The large shimpaku and low protein content of this rice mean that the residual rice will be sweeter than that of other sake rice varieties. Yauemon Junmai Nigori is rich yet not overly thick in texture, making it an excellent complement to spicy dishes when served chilled.

Iced Nigori Tea
Created by Ryu Okada

75ml	Gekkeikan nigori
75ml	Houjicha Infused oat milk
15ml	Maple syrup

Glass:	Rocks
Method:	Shake & Strain
Ice:	Cubed
Garnish:	Miso powder

Comments:
Dried miso powder is a fantastic addition here, as the umami of Nigori and miso blend together wonderfully to create a remarkably rich drink

Houjicha infused Oat Milk
100ml	Oat milk
2g	Loose Houjicha Tea

Add ingredients to a pan and bring to a boil. Let simmer for a few minutes, strain mixture and allow to cool before using.

Miso Powder:
Spread miso paste thinly and evenly on a baking tray. Place it in a dehydrator set to medium heat and dehydrate it until the miso can easily be broken up and ground into a powder using a pestle and mortar.

About this sake

The Gekkeikan Sake Company is a manufacturer of sake and plum wine. It was founded in 1637 by Jiemon Ōkura, the founder of Gekkeikan, who established the sake brewery in the town of Fushimi, renowned for its high-quality water. Gekkeikan is now one of Japan's oldest companies, with a name that literally means "laurel wreath." The sake produced by Gekkeikan is known for its characteristic sweetness and creamy medium-body. It exhibits hints of honey and tropical fruit aromas and flavours that culminate in a long-lasting finish.

Muroka Nama Genshu

Muroka (無濾過) - Unfiltered
Nama (生) - Unpasteurised
Genshu (原酒) - Undiluted

Muroka Nama Genshu Sake is not a widely seen sake style in the past 100 years, but it is gaining popularity worldwide as we speak. This style of sake is actually a blend of three different Japanese sake styles. Below, I'll break down these terms to help you understand what each of them means, and afterwards, we'll discuss this style of sake as a whole.

Muroka refers to a type of sake that has not been charcoal-filtered or fined. In the sake making process, charcoal filtration/fining is often used to remove impurities and enhance clarity. Muroka sake skips this filtration step, allowing it to retain more of its natural flavours and aromas. It tends to be slightly coloured but not always.

Nama means "raw" or "unpasteurised." Nama sake is not heat-treated or pasteurised after fermentation. Pasteurising sake is very similar to cooking garlic. Just as raw garlic is bold, hot, and overpowering, cooked garlic becomes sweet, subtle, and palatable. Sake follows a similar pattern, retaining more of its bold, funky, and "juicier" flavours when unpasteurised. Nama sake can come in various forms, including Nama, Nama Chozo, and Nama-Zume, each produced differently and affecting the sake differently. Because Nama sake is unpasteurised, it has a shorter shelf life compared to pasteurised sake and needs to be stored at cooler temperatures, which is why it can be harder to find globally than other sake styles.

Genshu is undiluted sake. Most sake is diluted with water before bottling to adjust its alcohol content to a socially preferred ABV, typically around 15%. This doesn't mean Genshu sake will have a higher ABV, often it's fermented to the typically 15-16%, but it can be seen to bottled around 18-20%. Generally, Genshu sake is richer and more intense than sake diluted with water.

While you may encounter these terms individually on various sake bottles, the Muroka Nama Genshu style is gaining prominence on its own. While I hesitate to compare sake to natural wine, it's akin to "lower intervention" sake. It combines the intense flavours of Genshu with the less refined Muroka and the bold, strong flavours of Nama. The result is a powerful and bold sake.

For mixing, it's a treasure trove of flavours. If you've struggled to taste sake in mixed drinks before, try using Muroka Nama Genshu, and you'll notice the difference.

Fun Fact
This is where sake names can become extremely long. It wouldn't be unusual to come across a sake bottle labelled "Junmai Daiginjo Goyakumangoku Yamahai Muroka Nama Genshu." In fact, one of my favourite bottles that I get each year is a "Gozenshu Junmai Omachi Bodaimoto Usu-nigori Namazake."

A Great Example

Brewery: Noguchi Naohiko Sake Institute
Prefecture: Isikawa
Bottle Name: Junmai Daiginjo 2018 Vintage
Style: Junmai Daiginjo Muroka Nama Genshu
Rice: Hyogo Yamada Nishiki
Polishing: 50%

Mr. Noguchi Naohiko, an illustrious figure known as "The God of Sake Brewing" and a revered Toji, began his remarkable journey of sake production in 1949. Fast forward to 2017, he solidified his already extensive legacy by establishing the Noguchi Naohiko Sake Institute (NNSI). His vision was to pass on not only his expertise but also his very spirit and sake philosophy to the next generation of brewers.

Noguchi Naohiko Sake is championing the historic craft of Yamahai brewing, which he helped breathe new life into as the technique was fading away. They defy convention by aging unpasteurised sake, showcasing its evolution as it matures, revealing the intricate complexities that most brewers would not allow to develop.

Located in Ishikawa Prefecture, where they draw from the crystal-clear, medium-hard snowmelt waters of Mt. Hakusan. They use an array of rice varieties from all over Japan, aiming to create sakes that capture the essence of each grain. At Noguchi Naohiko Sake Institute, the pursuit of quality is unyielding, epitomised by one of my all-time favourite sakes, the Junmai Daiginjo 2018 Vintage. With each sip, it unfolds a kaleidoscope of aromas and flavours, from exotic tropical fruits to the ripest tomatoes. Its balance is a revelation—velvet in texture with a lingering, transcendental finish. Whether savoured in solitude or alongside robust dishes, this sake is nothing short of an awe-inspiring masterpiece, a testament to the boundless possibilities of the craft.

Namabaldi
Created by Samuel Boulton

40ml	Sankou Hinokuchi Honjozo Nama Genshu
20ml	Nardini Bitter
100ml	Fresh Orange Juice

Glass:	Highball
Method:	Build
Ice:	Cubed
Garnish:	Fresh Orange Wedge

Comments:
The classic Italian cocktail, a Garibaldi, is a masterpiece in simplicity behind a bar, combining just two ingredients: Campari and orange juice. However, this specification calls for three ingredients. I used Nardini Bitter instead of Campari, as it's slightly sweeter, but you can use Campari and add sugar to taste if you prefer. This Nama is very punchy, so it remains distinct amidst the acidic and bitter ingredients.

About this sake
Sankou Hinokuchi is a Honjozo Nama Genshu from Sanko Masamune in Okayama Prefecture. "Hinokuchi" refers to the spout on the side of the sake filtering machine, indicating that this sake is in its purest form immediately after filtration, Nama and Genshu. It's a burst of energy, excitement, and vitality!
It has flavours of juicy melon, ripe pear, tropical pineapple, and creamy banana, complemented by zesty lemon peel, tangy grapefruit, and crisp red apple notes. All of these flavours are enriched by a deep umami complexity and hints of dried fruits. Best enjoyed when served chilled.

Ladybug
Created by Klára Kopčiková

50ml	Sankou Hinokuchi Honjozo Nama Genshu
5ml	Coconut oil washed Chocolate Absinthe
10ml	Creme de Cacao
15ml	Black Tea Concentrate
5ml	60:40 Sugar syrup

Glass:	Coupettini
Method:	Stirred
Ice:	None
Garnish:	Fresh Orange Zest

Comments:
This drink was created by Klára Kopčiková for this book.

Coconut oil washed Chocolate Absinthe

50g	Coconut Oil (Warmed)
50g	Chocolate Absinthe

Combine warmed coconut oil with 50g of Chocolate absinthe. Let the mixture infuse for 5 hours at room temperature. Then, place it in the fridge and allow it to solidify. Finally, strain and bottle it.

Black Tea Concentrate

4 bags	Black Tea
200ml	Water

Cold brew 4 bags of black tea in 200ml water for 10 minutes.

About this sake

Sankou Hinokuchi is a Honjozo Nama Genshu from Sanko Masamune in Okayama Prefecture. "Hinokuchi" refers to the spout on the side of the sake filtering machine, indicating that this sake is in its purest form immediately after filtration: Nama and Genshu. It's a burst of energy, excitement, and vitality!

It has flavours of juicy melon, ripe pear, tropical pineapple, and creamy banana, complemented by zesty lemon peel, tangy grapefruit, and crisp red apple notes. All of these flavours are enriched by a deep umami complexity and hints of dried fruits. Best enjoyed when served chilled.

Ginger Nama Genshu
Created by Unknown - Tippsysake.com

30ml	Narutotai "Ginjo" Nama Genshu
30ml	Domaine de Canton
7.5ml	Fresh Ginger Juice
7.5ml	Fresh Lemon Juice

Glass:	Rocks
Method:	Stirred
Ice:	Cubed
Garnish:	Candied Ginger

Comments:
This cocktail was first featured on tippsysake.com. They had to say "This cocktail balances the desirable acidic and herbaceous flavours of Narutotai "Ginjo" Nama Genshu with sweet and warming ginger liqueur. Adding equal parts lemon and ginger juice helps to open up the undiluted genshu while maintaining the balanced calmness of this cocktail."

About this sake:
Narutotai Ginjo Nama Genshu from Honke Matsuura featured in 'Blade Runner 2049'. This sake boasts a vibrant character, overflowing with a pleasant acidity like yogurt with roasted hazelnuts, and even a touch of rice pudding. It is undiluted and unpasteurised finally bottled in a UV-protective aluminium containers.

Sparkling Sake

Sparkling Sake - 泡酒 (awa = bubbles so translates to bubbly sake)

Sparkling Sake has only been made in Japan for around 20 years. As a relatively new category of sake, a consistent style has not yet emerged. That being said, the field is full of creativity, meaning every sparkling sake is different and exciting.

Sparkling sake, sometimes referred to as Awazake, only gained prominence when Shirakabegura Brewery, located in Nada, Hyogo, launched their sparkling sake, Mio. It can now be found all over Japan and has grown in popularity so much that in November 2016, The Japan Awasake Association was established by and for Japanese breweries producing sparkling sake. The aim of the association is to improve product quality, raise brand awareness, and expand into new markets. Only the products that comply with the strict association standards and pass their third-party quality control can receive the AWA sake certification (of course you can still product whatever you want, however you want without the certification).

Sparkling sake can be made by one of two methods: the traditional Champagne-style method of secondary fermentation in the bottle, and the contemporary CO_2 injection process. In the traditional method, much like with Champagne, sparkling sake begins with carefully selected high-quality sake as the base. In the case of sake, as you can't add any additional ingredients, more koji and yeast are typically added in place of the dosage used in Champagne. The majority of sparkling sakes that use this method typically opt not to disgorge, leaving the sediment in the bottle.

The CO_2 injection method is a modern alternative and is great for entry-priced sparkling sake. It starts with a well-crafted, clear sake, to which carbon dioxide (CO_2) is introduced under controlled conditions, giving it a lively effervescence, while preserving the sake's original characteristics. Sparkling sake created through CO_2 injection delivers a crisp and vibrant tasting experience. Neither method is correct or better; it purely depends on the sake. What this does provide is a plethora of flavours and styles, making it great for mixing.

A Great Example

Brewery: Yonetsuru Shuzo
Prefecture: Yamagata
Bottle Name: Yonetsuru Rosé Sparkling
Style: Sparkling
Rice: Unknown
Polishing: 65%

Established around 1700 during the Genroku era, Yonetsuru became a leading force in the local sake brewing industry, as documented in the Yamagata Prefecture Sake Brewer's Guide compiled in 1916. Yonetsuru pioneered the cultivation of high-quality sake rice locally and subsequently produced sake from it. In 1983, in cooperation with local farmers, they formed the "Takahata-machi Sake Rice Research Association." Today, approximately half of the rice shipped from the Jimoto area is dedicated to sake production.

The name "Yonetsuru" draws inspiration from the graceful posture of rice ears bowing in the field and a local legend known as the "Crane's Return of a Favour." It encapsulates the aspiration to create sake that conveys a sense of gratitude and sincerity. Guided by a philosophy that centres on the rice-growing process, their Japanese sake is crafted using locally sourced rice, resulting in a harmonious blend of aroma, taste, and sharpness.

The "rosé-colour" of their rosé-coloured sake is produced by using "red yeast," which imparts red pigments, along with carbon dioxide gas.

This innovative sake offers a light, sweet, and slightly sour profile, harnessing its distinctive acidity and low alcohol content. It exhibits a brilliant rose gold hue, accompanied by notes of cherry, strawberry, and cranberry candy, intertwined with a velvety porridge undertone.

This sake was awarded a gold medal in the sparkling category of the Sake division at the International Wine Challenge (IWC) 2022 and qualifies for the Yamagata GI.

Kintsugi
Created by Samuel Boulton

| 1 Scoop | Yuzu Sorbet |
| 75ml | Akashi Tai Sparkling Sake |

Glass:	Rocks
Method:	Build
Ice:	None
Garnish:	Gold Sprayed chocolate Butter

Comments:
This take on a Sgroppino is inspired by the art form of Kintsugi, which celebrates the concept of broken objects being repaired and becoming even more valuable. It was crafted for the Winter 2022 menu of Shibuya Underground in Birmingham, UK.

Yuzu Sorbet
600ml	Water
250g	Sugar
225ml	Yuzu Juice

Place everything in a blender. Blend until smooth. Pour mixture into a container and place in freezer.

About this sake
The Akashi-Tai Brewery, situated in the harbour town of Akashi in southwestern Japan, draws its name from this area and "Tai," which means fish. As sea bream can be seen challenging waters along Akashi's shoreline.

Made in a similar way as Champagne and other traditional method sparkling wines. It starts with a Ginjo Sake then undergoes a secondary fermentation in the bottle. This sake is slightly sweet with plenty of apple like acidity.

Sakura Season
Created by Samuel Boulton

50ml	Mancino Sakura Vermouth
60ml	Akashi Tai Sparkling Sake
25ml	Light Tonic Water

Glass:	Masu and Cup
Method:	Build - Sosogi-Koboshi
Ice:	None
Garnish:	None

Comments:
A lovely blend of Sakura and herbal flavours from the vermouth, mixed with the lovely apple and melon of the Akashi-Tai. This drink is light, VERY light. As this is built without ice, I would chill all ingredient before serving.

About this sake
The Akashi-Tai Brewery, situated in the harbour town of Akashi in southwestern Japan, draws its name from this area and "Tai," which means fish. As sea bream can be seen challenging waters along Akashi's shoreline.
Made in a similar way as Champagne and other traditional method sparkling wines starting with a Ginjo Sake then undergoes a secondary fermentation in the bottle. This sake is slightly sweet with plenty of apple like acidity.

Sgromio
Created by Samuel Boulton

| 1 Scoop | Midori Sorbet |
| 75ml | Mio Sparkling Sake |

Glass:	Rocks
Method:	Build
Ice:	None
Garnish:	None

Comments:
It's rare that I ever make two drinks of the same type like this, but Sgroppino is a great way to truly showcase a sparkling sake.

Midori Sorbet
600ml	Water
150g	Sugar
225ml	Midori

Place everything in a blender. Blend until smooth. Pour mixture into a container and place in freezer. If you struggle to get the Sorbet to set, add more water.

About this sake
Shirakabegura Brewery, located in Nada, Hyogo, launched their sparkling sake, Mio, which took Japan by storm. The now iconic little blue bottles can be seen in most alcohol stores in Japan. This sake is very apple heavy and leans on the sweet side.

Flavoured Sake

Flavoured sake is a variation of traditional Japanese sake. In this type of sake, additional flavours are intentionally added to the beverage to create a unique and distinctive product. These added flavours can come from a variety of sources and are meant to complement or enhance the natural characteristics of sake.

I'd like to clarify immediately that this category is very often misrepresented. The Kanji for alcohol, as already discussed, is 酒. This can be read in two ways, as *shu* or *sake*. Both mean alcohol. This means a bottle labelled Yuzushu to the untrained eye could be read as either Yuzu alcohol or Yuzu sake, even though there is no sake (nihonshu) in the bottle. This information shouldn't deter you from buying shochu or sake-based Yuzushu, but rather should help inform you. Many Yuzu "sake" are simply shochu-based with added sake for flavour (and marketing purposes).

As the category of flavoured sake includes additional flavourings, it doesn't conform to any grading system and is open to having artificial ingredients/flavourings and sugars, etc, added. Additionally, flavoured sake can be produced in numerous ways, with most varieties infused with a wide range of ingredients. Common flavourings usually involve fruits, such as plum, peach, or cherry, but spices such as ginger and cinnamon are also seen. You can even find yogurt flavour.

The production process for flavoured sake varies depending on the desired outcome. In some cases, producers will use artificial flavourings, others, the flavouring ingredients are added during the brewing process, while most, will macerated post-fermentation. The sake is typically filtered to remove any solid particles or residue, but premium producers may leave solids in the bottle if they believe this adds to the enjoyment. Flavoured sake can range in sweetness levels, from dry to very sweet, depending on the amount of added sugar or sweet flavourings. Some flavoured sakes are quite sweet, making them popular choices alongside desserts.

The most common of these is Umeshu. Ume (or plum) fruit is grow in huge abundance in Japan but only have a short (few-week) window in which they are in season. So, to not have waste, the Japanese people have developed many ways over the years of preserving them for year-round enjoyment. One of these is Umeshu, which can be legally made at home or at an Izakaya. Ume are picked (typically out of season) unripe and added to a clear alcohol base, like shochu, to draw out the flavour. As these are unripe Ume, they are quite sour, so a ton of sugar is added to balance it out. This is why most Umeshu is very sweet. It also explains why you can find homemade Umeshu all around Japan!

A few common types of flavoured sake/shochu liqueurs are:

Umeshu: Plum sake, made by infusing sake with Japanese plums and sugar. It has a sweet and fruity plum flavour.

Yuzu sake: Yuzu is a citrus fruit (chemically a cross between a lemon, mandarine, and grapefruit). Yuzu sake is made by infusing sake with the zest and juice of yuzu. It has a bright, citrusy flavour. When buying Yuzushu, always look for a bottle with remaining sediment. The majority of Yuzu's flavour comes from the oils in the skin, not the juice so filtering these out will hugely reduce the product's kick.

Ginger sake: Sake infused with ginger, which imparts a spicy and aromatic quality. Typically ginger from the Kochi region is used, as it is regarded as the best in Japan.

The category of flavoured sake is quite fascinating, and the combinations are nearly endless. You can find everything from Nigori Strawberry sake to Sparkling Yuzushu. All of these flavoured options are excellent for mixing because they carry the flavour of their fruit/spice alongside some umami-rich sake notes. It is worth noting as well, that as these products contain flavour and sugar, they are typically used as additions to cocktails rather than as the base. The recipes below reflect this.

For this section, I won't be showcasing a specific example as there is such a wide variety in what constitutes flavoured sake. Instead, consider some specifications using Umeshu, Yuzushu, and a few other flavoured options.

Umeshu Cup
Created by Samuel Boulton

50ml	Umeshu
Top	Ginger Ale

Glass:	Highball
Method:	Build
Ice:	Cubed
Garnish:	Orange wedge, mint and strawberries

Comments:
A simple take on the British Pimm's Cup. This isn't an exciting drink, but mixing with Umeshu can sometimes get very complicated for bartenders. Make yourself one of these, put down the sesame seeds, and chill out. Creatively can be simple sometimes.

About this Sake
Don't worry about this one, use what you have and enjoy.

Dessert
Created by Beau Price

75ml	Kodakara Umeshu
5ml	Suze
5ml	Acid Mix
50ml	Ginger Ale

Glass:	Wine
Method:	Build
Ice:	None
Garnish:	Japanese Tag

Comments:
Made for the opening menu of Shibuya Underground in Birmingham, UK, by bartender Beau Price. This drink is a hymn to what Umeshu can be: light, delicate, slightly bitter and sour thanks to the acids and Suze. A great way to introduce someone to Umeshu!

Acid Mix
94g	Filtered Water
4g	Citric Acid Powder
2g	Malic Acid Powder

Place everything in a container and stir until acids are dissolved.

About this sake
Crafted by the Junmai Daiginjo experts at Tatenokawa Shuzo, it begins with the selection of the finest Nanko plums gathered

from the bountiful orchards of Yamagata Prefecture. These plums are then blended with Tatenokawa Junmai Daiginjo sake and a Shochu derived from the Kasu (lees) of the same sake, along with a touch of sugar. The outcome is a luscious, sweet profile that gracefully counterbalances the inherent tartness of the plums.

Lychee and Sake Spritz
Created by Tony Kousoulou

40ml	Akashi-Tai Umeshu
20ml	Monin Lychee syrup
80ml	Champagne
10ml	Citric blend (1:9)
2 Drops	20% Saline solution

Glass:	Flute
Method:	Build
Ice:	None
Garnish:	Dehydrated grapefruit slice and apple blossom

Comments:
Created as a sake twist on a French 75-style cocktail, Tony discovered that the plum undertones of the sake complemented lychee, a relative in the stone fruit family. Therefore, chose to use a flavoured syrup instead of a standard one. This decision was also made to attract a wider audience and introduce them to sake-based cocktails.

About this sake
A product made by the UK's best known sake brewery, Akashi-Tai. This Umeshu is shochu-based Umeshu with added Ginjo sake. This Umeshu has a noticeably sweet and tangy profile. These combined make this sake ideal for cocktails.

Demon
Created by Klára Kopčiková

50ml	Kodakara Daiginjo Umeshu
20ml	Salted caramel
25ml	Cafe Borghetti
2 Dash	Angostura bitters

Glass:	Nick and Nora
Method:	Stirred
Ice:	None
Garnish:	Chocolate covered strawberry stick

Comments:
This drink was apart of a 5 course drinks only tasting event and was never design to be drank alone. The event was themed around the Studio Ghibli film, Princess Mononoke. During the film Prince Ashitaka encounters a demon, who puts his village in danger. Ashitaka kills him, but a small piece of darkness attaches to his arm, which might eventually lead to his death. After the demon dies, we learn that the darkness had attached to a host, a large hog. Ashitaka has to leave his village and his people to save himself. The drink is inspired by the darkness of the demon.

About this sake
This Umeshu was specially imported for Shibuya Underground. Made by steeping Nanko plums in a base of Tatenokawa Daiginjo sake, this umeshu is rich and indulgent with a lovely acidity. It was also the winner of the 2010 Tenman Tenshin Plum Wine Championships.

Yuzu Snowball
Created by Samuel Boulton

50ml	Advocaat
20ml	Akashi Tai Yuzushu
Top	Lemonade

Glass:	Highball
Method:	Build
Ice:	Cubed
Garnish:	Grated nutmeg

Comments:
Perhaps another super simple spec, but a great one. A take on another classic British drink (a Christmas favourite of the author). This spec merely replaces the classic lime cordial with Yuzushu but is a great example of how Japanese flavours can integrate with Western classics.

About this sake:
Akashi Tai Yuzushu is shochu-based Yuzushu with added Ginjo sake. This Yuzushu is noticeably sharp and more "juicy" than most others. The sharpness of this sake makes it great for mixing but requires ice or soda to enjoy on its own.

Bee Corp
Created by Gergő Muráth

40ml	Sipsmith Lemon Drizzle gin
15ml	Akashi Tai Yuzushu
15ml	Rosemary and orange blossom honey syrup
20ml	Fresh tangerine juice

Glass:	Coup
Method:	Shake
Ice:	None
Garnish:	Orange Peel

Comments:
This cocktail was crafted exclusively for the VIP hospitality suite at Wimbledon 2023. To provide a bit of context, it's worth noting that Sipsmith holds a B-Corp certification. Thus, the name cleverly pays homage to the classic "Bee's Knees" cocktail, which served as the initial inspiration for this unique creation.

Rosemary and Orange Blossom Honey:

500g	Honey
250g	Water
4	Rosemary Sprigs
50ml	Orange Blossom Water

Gently warm 500g of honey, 250g of water, and four sprigs of fresh rosemary in a saucepan until combined. Once mixed, remove the saucepan from the heat and let the infuse for a minimum of 20 minutes. After the infusion period, strain out the rosemary. Finally add, 50ml of orange blossom water.

About this sake
Akashi Tai Yuzushu is Shochu-based Yuzushu with added Ginjo Sake. This Yuzushu is noticeably sharp and more "juicy" than most others. The sharpness of this sake makes it great for mixing but requires ice or soda to enjoy on its own.

Yuzu Cooler
Created by Jack Chalk

30ml	Hendricks Gin
25ml	Cucumber Cordial
25ml	Monin Coconut Syrup
20ml	Akashi-Tai Yuzushu
Top	Soda

Glass:	Highball
Method:	Swizzle
Ice:	Crushed
Garnish:	Large lemon wedge coconut chunk & mint

Comments:
This drink was crafted for a special menu featuring Hendrick's Gin. Given the theme of Hendrick's Gin, the inclusion of homemade cucumber cordial was an obvious choice. Jack immediately recognised that Yuzushu would work beautifully with coconut and cucumber.
He approached the creation of this drink as a unique twist on a Mojito, with the goal of allowing yuzu to shine as the star ingredient. While ensuring a citrusy balance, it added an extra layer of zesty vibrancy and complexity that couldn't be replicated by any other citrus-focused component. As a result, it became a popular summer sensation, selling out in no time!

Cucumber Cordial:

500g	Cucumber
100g	Caster sugar

| 100g | Fructose |
| 5g | Citric Acid |

Juice Cucumbers and strain liquid. Add fructose, caster sugar and citric acid and stir until dissolved.

About this sake
Akashi Tai Yuzushu is Shochu-based Yuzushu with added Ginjo Sake. This Yuzushu is noticeably sharp and more "juicy" than most others. The sharpness of this sake makes it great for mixing but requires ice or soda to enjoy on its own.

Basil Fawlty
Created by Samuel Boulton

40ml	Homare Strawberry Nigori
25ml	Fino Sherry
3	Basil Leaf
10ml	2:1 Sugar Syrup
25ml	Cloudy Apple Juice
25ml	Pomegranate Juice

Glass:	Wine
Method:	Shake & Fine Strain
Ice:	Cubed
Garnish:	Jasmine Flower

Comments:
This drink was originally conceived in 2016 as part of a movie-themed takeover at 40 St Pauls, which would later earn the prestigious title of World Gin Bar of the Year in 2019, this drink has now been revitalised for inclusion in this book. It now features a fresh Strawberry Nigorizake.

My firsthand encounter with strawberry sake occurred during my visit to Hyogo at Akashi-Tai, where the town of Akashi is renowned for its exceptional strawberries. They are artfully blended with fresh sake, resulting in a delightful enjoyable sake. If you haven't had the pleasure of experiencing strawberry sake, I highly recommend giving it a try.

About this sake
Although the Akashi-Tai Strawberry sake is exclusively found in the local Akashi area. We are lucky to have Homare

Strawberry! This exceptional blend harmoniously marries the mellowness, sweetness, and full-bodied essence of unfiltered nigori sake with the invigoratingly tangy and sweet notes of strawberries, resulting in a truly exquisite fusion of flavours.

C.R.E.A.M. & C.O.O.K.I.E.S
Created by Samuel Boulton

30ml	H by Hine
40ml	Homare Chocolate Nigori
10ml	Giffard Cookies Syrup
1 Dash	Tonka Bean Essence

Glass:	Rocks
Method:	Shake & Strain
Ice:	Block Ice
Garnish:	Mini Cookie

Comments:
This drink was originally designed with cream liqueur and later adapted to feature Chocolate Nigori.

About this sake
Homare Chocolate is a lovely mix of creamy nigori sake and a high quality chocolate sauce. It shouldn't taste as good as it does!

Lycheeni
Created by Samuel Boulton & Klára Kopčiková

20ml	Koskenkorva Blueberry Vodka
30ml	Homare Lychee Nigori
25ml	Rubicon Lychee juice
5ml	Giiffard Raspberry syrup
2 dash	Spanish Bitters

Glass:	Nic&Nora
Method:	Shake and Fine Strain
Ice:	None
Garnish:	Leopard Print Material

Comments:
This drink was original a take on the classic Lychee Martini by Klára Kopčiková and was then adapted by Samuel Boulton for this book.

About this sake
Homare Lychee is a lovely mix of junmai nigori sake and a high quality Lychee Puree. Fresh and fruit with a lovely creaminess.

Other Sake Styles

In the previous sections, we have covered a wide range of common sake styles, but there is still more to explore. While I can't delve into all styles in detail, there are certainly some worth your attention. The world of sake is vast and continually evolving. If you're eager to expand your knowledge, I encourage you to explore these omitted styles, each with its unique flavours and traditions.

Doburoku (濁酒) is a rustic, traditional, and often homemade style of rice drink, that remains unfiltered, boasting a distinctively rich and sweet taste.

Doburoku is a traditional Japanese beverage that was regularly brewed at home. However, it was banned during the Meiji era when the Japanese government introduced measures to regulate alcohol production and taxation.

In recent years, Doburoku has seen a resurgence in popularity, and with many commercial producers entering the market. It distinguishes itself from other sakes with its thicker and sweeter and tangy composition, but it significantly varies from bottle to bottle. While it may initially resemble Nigori sake, Doburoku holds its own unique characteristics.

Typically, Doburoku has a lower alcohol content compared to Nihonshu. In the brewing process of Doburoku, all ingredients are added simultaneously, unlike the stepped processes used in traditional sake production. Consequently, the yeast in the fermenting mixture does not have ample time to multiply, as it would in a regular batch. As the koji breaks down the starches in the rice, the yeast becomes overwhelmed by the substantial amount of sugar generated. The yeast produced is insufficient to convert much of the sugar into alcohol. The fermentation process is then halted naturally, as the sugar essentially kills off the yeast, resulting in a tangy beverage with a lower alcohol content.

Taru (樽酒): Taru sake is aged in cedar barrels, imparting a woody and slightly floral flavour to the sake. It's important to note that while the term "aged" is commonly used, a more accurate description is "finished." This sake only spends 2-3 weeks in cedar wood barrels at the end of its production.
Japanese cedar, scientifically known as Cryptomeria japonica, is a large evergreen tree native to Japan and belongs to the cypress family.

Historically, sake production was centred in Hyogo prefecture, close to the old capital, Kyoto. However, when the capital moved from Kyoto to Edo (now Tokyo), it meant a longer travel time for sake to reach consumers at the start of the season. The first to arrive with sake could demand premium prices because thirsty patrons were willing to pay extra. This created a competitive race along the Nakasendo trail, connecting Kyoto to Edo. Transporting sake in clay vessels over long distances was risky due to the potential for cracking, so wooden barrels were used to move the sake.

Eventually, the faster sea route replaced overland travel, and the practice of using cedar barrels ceased. Today, Taruzake is made to honour the 2-3 week journey sake would have taken from Kyoto to Edo.

Kijoshu (貴醸酒): Kijoshu is a luxurious and less common sake style made by replacing a portion of the water used in the brewing process with sake itself. This results in a sweeter, more concentrated sake with a complex profile.

Kijoshu has a higher sugar content than regular sake, making it richer and sweeter. While it may not reach the sweetness levels of a dessert wine, Kijoshu can be used in similar contexts.

Sake Tasting Pages
Please uses these pages to document any sake you've tried while reading this book.

Sake Name	....	Rice	....
Prefecture	....	Polishing	....
		ABV	....
Brewery	....	Yeast	....
		GI/App	....

Rating ☆☆☆☆☆

Grade:

☐ Futsu-shu

☐ Junmai
☐ Tokubetsu Junmai
☐ Junmai Ginjo
☐ Junmai Daiginjo

☐ Honjozo
☐ Tokubetsu Honjozo
☐ Ginjo
☐ Daiginjo

Starters
☐ Sokujo
☐ Bodaimoto
☐ Mizumoto
☐ Kimoto
☐ Yamahai
☐ Unknown

Other:
☐ Muroka
☐ Genshu
☐ Taru
☐ Nama
☐ Nigori
☐ Sparkling
☐ Other ....

Notes:

_____

_____

_____

_____

SMV ....

Amino ....

Acidity ....

Price ....

Food Pairing

_____

Temperature
Very Chilled   Chilled   Ambient   Warm   Hot

Sake Name	....	Rice Polishing ....
Prefecture	....	ABV ....
		Yeast ....
Brewery	....	GI/App ....

Rating ☆☆☆☆☆

Grade:

☐ Junmai
☐ Tokubetsu Junmai
☐ Junmai Ginjo
☐ Junmai Daiginjo

☐ Futsu-shu
☐ Honjozo
☐ Tokubetsu Honjozo
☐ Ginjo
☐ Daiginjo

Starters
☐ Sokujo
☐ Bodaimoto
☐ Mizumoto
☐ Kimoto
☐ Yamahai
☐ Unknown

Other:
☐ Muroka
☐ Genshu
☐ Taru
☐ Nama
☐ Nigori
☐ Sparkling
☐ Other ....

Notes:

_____

_____

_____

_____

SMV ....

Amino ....

Acidity ....

Price ....

Food Pairing

_____

Temperature

Very Chilled   Chilled   Ambient   Warm   Hot

Sake Name	....	Rice Polishing	....
Prefecture	....	ABV	....
		Yeast	....
Brewery	....	GI/App	....

Rating ☆☆☆☆☆

Grade:

- ☐ Futsu-shu
- ☐ Junmai
- ☐ Honjozo
- ☐ Tokubetsu Junmai
- ☐ Tokubetsu Honjozo
- ☐ Junmai Ginjo
- ☐ Ginjo
- ☐ Junmai Daiginjo
- ☐ Daiginjo

Starters
- ☐ Sokujo
- ☐ Bodaimoto
- ☐ Mizumoto
- ☐ Kimoto
- ☐ Yamahai
- ☐ Unknown

Other:
- ☐ Muroka
- ☐ Genshu
- ☐ Taru
- ☐ Nama
- ☐ Nigori
- ☐ Sparkling
- ☐ Other ....

Notes:
_____
_____
_____
_____

SMV ....
Amino ....
Acidity ....

Price ....

Food Pairing
_____

Temperature
Very Chilled   Chilled   Ambient   Warm   Hot

Sake Name	....	Rice Polishing	....
Prefecture	....	ABV	....
		Yeast	....
Brewery	....	GI/App	....

Rating ☆☆☆☆☆

Grade:

- ☐ Futsu-shu
- ☐ Junmai
- ☐ Honjozo
- ☐ Tokubetsu Junmai
- ☐ Tokubetsu Honjozo
- ☐ Junmai Ginjo
- ☐ Ginjo
- ☐ Junmai Daiginjo
- ☐ Daiginjo

Starters
- ☐ Sokujo
- ☐ Bodaimoto
- ☐ Mizumoto
- ☐ Kimoto
- ☐ Yamahai
- ☐ Unknown

Other:
- ☐ Muroka
- ☐ Genshu
- ☐ Taru
- ☐ Nama
- ☐ Nigori
- ☐ Sparkling
- ☐ Other ....

Notes:
_____
_____
_____
_____

SMV ....

Amino ....

Acidity ....

Price ....

Food Pairing
_____

Temperature
Very Chilled   Chilled   Ambient   Warm   Hot

Sake Name	....	Rice ....
		Polishing ....
Prefecture	....	ABV ....
		Yeast ....
Brewery	....	GI/App ....

Rating ☆☆☆☆☆

Grade:

☐ Futsu-shu

☐ Junmai
☐ Tokubetsu Junmai
☐ Junmai Ginjo
☐ Junmai Daiginjo

☐ Honjozo
☐ Tokubetsu Honjozo
☐ Ginjo
☐ Daiginjo

Starters
☐ Sokujo
☐ Bodaimoto
☐ Mizumoto
☐ Kimoto
☐ Yamahai
☐ Unknown

Other:
☐ Muroka
☐ Genshu
☐ Taru
☐ Nama
☐ Nigori
☐ Sparkling
☐ Other ....

Notes:

_____
_____
_____
_____

SMV ....

Amino ....

Acidity ....

Price ....

Food Pairing

_____

Temperature
Very Chilled   Chilled   Ambient   Warm   Hot

Sake Name	....	Rice Polishing	....
Prefecture	....	ABV	....
		Yeast	....
Brewery	....	GI/App	....

Rating ☆☆☆☆☆

Grade:

☐ Junmai
☐ Tokubetsu Junmai
☐ Junmai Ginjo
☐ Junmai Daiginjo

☐ Futsu-shu
☐ Honjozo
☐ Tokubetsu Honjozo
☐ Ginjo
☐ Daiginjo

Starters
☐ Sokujo
☐ Bodaimoto
☐ Mizumoto
☐ Kimoto
☐ Yamahai
☐ Unknown

Other:
☐ Muroka
☐ Genshu
☐ Taru
☐ Nama
☐ Nigori
☐ Sparkling
☐ Other   ....

Notes:
_____
_____
_____
_____

SMV   ....

Amino ....

Acidity ....

Price   ....

Food Pairing

_____

Temperature
Very Chilled   Chilled   Ambient   Warm   Hot

Sake Name	....	Rice	....
		Polishing	....
Prefecture	....	ABV	....
		Yeast	....
Brewery	....	GI/App	....

Rating ☆☆☆☆☆

Grade:

☐ Futsu-shu
☐ Junmai   ☐ Honjozo
☐ Tokubetsu Junmai   ☐ Tokubetsu Honjozo
☐ Junmai Ginjo   ☐ Ginjo
☐ Junmai Daiginjo   ☐ Daiginjo

Starters   Other:
☐ Sokujo   ☐ Muroka
☐ Bodaimoto   ☐ Genshu
☐ Mizumoto   ☐ Taru
☐ Kimoto   ☐ Nama
☐ Yamahai   ☐ Nigori
☐ Unknown   ☐ Sparkling
                 ☐ Other   ....

Notes:

_____

_____

_____

_____

SMV ....

Amino ....

Acidity ....

Price ....

Food Pairing
_____

Temperature
Very Chilled   Chilled   Ambient   Warm   Hot

Sake Name	....	Rice Polishing	....
			....
Prefecture	....	ABV	....
		Yeast	....
Brewery	....	GI/App	....

Rating ☆☆☆☆☆

Grade:

☐ Futsu-shu
☐ Junmai
☐ Tokubetsu Junmai
☐ Junmai Ginjo
☐ Junmai Daiginjo

☐ Futsu-shu
☐ Honjozo
☐ Tokubetsu Honjozo
☐ Ginjo
☐ Daiginjo

Starters
☐ Sokujo
☐ Bodaimoto
☐ Mizumoto
☐ Kimoto
☐ Yamahai
☐ Unknown

Other:
☐ Muroka
☐ Genshu
☐ Taru
☐ Nama
☐ Nigori
☐ Sparkling
☐ Other ....

Notes:

_____

_____

_____

_____

SMV ....

Amino ....

Acidity ....

Price ....

Food Pairing
_____

Temperature
Very Chilled   Chilled   Ambient   Warm   Hot

Sake Name	....	Rice	....
Prefecture	....	Polishing	....
		ABV	....
Brewery	....	Yeast	....
		GI/App	....

Rating ☆☆☆☆☆

Grade:

☐ Futsu-shu
☐ Junmai   ☐ Honjozo
☐ Tokubetsu Junmai   ☐ Tokubetsu Honjozo
☐ Junmai Ginjo   ☐ Ginjo
☐ Junmai Daiginjo   ☐ Daiginjo

Starters   Other:
☐ Sokujo   ☐ Muroka
☐ Bodaimoto   ☐ Genshu
☐ Mizumoto   ☐ Taru
☐ Kimoto   ☐ Nama
☐ Yamahai   ☐ Nigori
☐ Unknown   ☐ Sparkling
                            ☐ Other   ....

Notes:
_____

_____

_____

_____

SMV ....

Amino ....

Acidity ....

Price ....

Food Pairing
_____

Temperature
Very Chilled   Chilled   Ambient   Warm   Hot

Sake Name	....	Rice Polishing	....

Sake Name ....   Rice Polishing ....

Prefecture ....   ABV ....

   Yeast ....

Brewery ....   GI/App ....

Rating ☆☆☆☆☆

Grade:

□ Futsu-shu

□ Junmai   □ Honjozo

□ Tokubetsu Junmai   □ Tokubetsu Honjozo

□ Junmai Ginjo   □ Ginjo

□ Junmai Daiginjo   □ Daiginjo

Starters   Other:

□ Sokujo   □ Muroka

□ Bodaimoto   □ Genshu

□ Mizumoto   □ Taru

□ Kimoto   □ Nama

□ Yamahai   □ Nigori

□ Unknown   □ Sparkling

   □ Other ....

Notes:

_____

_____

_____

_____

SMV ....

Amino ....

Acidity ....

Price ....

Food Pairing

_____

Temperature

Very Chilled   Chilled   Ambient   Warm   Hot

CHAPTER FIVE
SHOCHU

Shochu
/Show-Chu/

1. A Japanese spirit distilled from various base materials, known for its distinct umami flavour and lower alcohol content.

Shochu Introduction

Shochu is a beloved beverage in Japan with historic roots and a somewhat mysterious origin story. Multiple theories abound regarding its journey to Japan. One suggests it arrived from China via the East China Sea, while the most widely accepted theory states that Shochu made its debut in Ryukyu after originating in Thailand on the Indochina Peninsula.

It's commonly accepted that Portuguese missionaries brought distillation technology with them. This is backed up by historical records from the Joseon era (present-day Korea) that state a distilled liquor known as Awamori was already being crafted in Ryukyu as early as 1477, marking it as Japan's inaugural distilled spirit. In 1546, a Portuguese visitor to Japan documented something describing a spirit as "distilled liquor made from rice." Over time, as the value of rice grew, locals opted to use other ingredients, including potatoes and barley as the base of their shochu, as rice was needed to pay their taxes.

The first recorded use of the word "shochu" in Japan dates back to a remarkable historical find. In 1954, a wooden piece was discovered in the roof of the Koriyama Hachiman Shrine in Oguchi City, Kagoshima. This artefact, dating back to August 21st, 1559, bears an inscription that sheds light on the context of that time. It reads, "The monk was so stingy, he did not offer us any shochu," and it was signed by two disgruntled builders who were involved in the renovation of the shrine. This fascinating discovery not only provides insight into the early use of the term "shochu" but also offers a glimpse into the historical significance of shochu.

Modern-day Shochu is a Japanese distilled spirit typically made from a range of base ingredients, including barley, sweet potatoes, rice, and sugar. It is a well-loved alcoholic beverage in Japan, renowned for its comparatively lower alcohol content in comparison to spirits such as vodka or whiskey. Typically, Shochu has an alcohol content ranging from about 25% to 40%, although this can vary. Before delving into more details about Shochu, I'd like to explain something first.

Soju vs Shochu

In the previous paragraphs, I mentioned Korea, and it's likely that many people are familiar with the Korean national drink, Soju. While I do not profess to be an expert on soju, I will quickly dispel any misconceptions about the two as it is common for the two to be mixed up.

Korean soju is a clear, distilled alcoholic beverage that is one of the most popular and iconic spirits from South Korea.

Traditionally, soju was made from grains like rice, wheat, or barley. However, in recent years, many commercial varieties use other ingredients like sweet potatoes or tapioca. These variations can give soju slightly different flavours and characteristics however almost all are highly rectified, removing most distinguishable characteristics

Soju is known for its relatively high alcohol content (compared to other table drinks, like wine), typically ranging from 16% to 25% ABV. There are lower-alcohol versions more commonly available internationally, which are normally flavoured and have an alcohol content of around 13%.

None flavoured soju has a neutral and somewhat sweet flavour, which makes it easy to drink and great for mixing in cocktails. It lacks the strong, distinctive flavours of some other spirits, such as whiskey or rum, and of course, Honkaku shochu.

Soju is typically made to keep the cost of the product as low as possible, which often means using artificial or commercial scale ingredients and industrial practices. This being said, artisan producers are reemerging.

Soju is typically served chilled in small glasses. It is often enjoyed in a group setting. As eating in Korea is a social activity, it is very common to order two or three bottles of soju at a time for the whole table to enjoy.

There are several brands of soju available in Korea, with Jinro (pronounced ji-lo) being one of the most well-known and widely consumed around the world.

South Korea has strict regulations on the production and sale of soju, including limitations on alcohol content, bottle size, and pricing, to control its consumption. Korean soju is not only popular domestically but has also gained some international recognition due to its unique characteristics and its role in Korean pop culture. Soju is seeing a high rise in popularity in America among younger drinkers due to its low cost and ease of consumption.

I implore you to try soju. While it's not a personal favourite of mine like Japanese shochu is, soju is a fun drink. Below, I've included some recipes using soju for those wanting to explore and try.

Note: It is possible to sometimes see a bottle of Japanese shochu labelled as soju in western markets. I can't explain this better than how Christopher Pellegrini, one of the worlds leading shochu experts does in his book *The Shochu Handbook.*

"Due to state-specific American liquor control tax loopholes, many eating and drinking establishments in the US that carry Shochu, particular in California, serve it under the name Soju. It's Korean multiple-distilled cousin. In many cases it actually says 'Soju' right on the bottle. Obviously, this has had the effect of confusing and misinforming customers. The reason for this is Soju, due to its mid-level ABV and some heavy lobbying at the California state capital, now skirts the parameters of a full blown license liquor licenses, which can be prohibitively expensive for new business owners. Many establishments opt for the less restrictive beer and wine license which currently accommodates some medium ABV drinks like Soju (24% ABV and lower). Hence, Shochu has benefitted from hiding under the soju umbrella in a handful of key markets." - Christopher Pellegrini (The Shochu Handbook, 2014)

Bank Heist
Created by Ryan Smith

20ml	Calvados
20ml	Jameson Black Barrel
25ml	Muhak Good Day Red-Pomegranate Soju
25ml	Lime Juice
20ml	Port
5ml	1:1 Sugar syrup

Glass:	Coup
Method:	Shake & Fine Strain
Ice:	None
Garnish:	Grated nutmeg

Comments:
This cocktail was inspired by a bankers punch. It is an autumnal sour, with a fruity edge.

About this Soju
Smooth and fruity with a punch of sweet red pomegranate flavour. At 13.5% alcohol this crisp soju is refreshing to serve straight, with ice.

Peach
Created by Blaise Bachelier

25ml	Money Shoulder
25ml	Jinro Peach Soju
10ml	Lemon Juice
15ml	Orange and Almond Syrup
Dash	Peach Bitters

Glass:	Rocks
Method:	Shake & Fine Strain
Ice:	Cubed
Garnish:	

Comments:
This cocktail was created for this book.

Orange and Almond Syrup

60g	Orange Peel
60g	Almond Flakes
100g	Sugar
100g	Coconut Water

Let the sugar, orange and almond sit together for an hour, in an airtight container as if you were making an oleo.
Add the coconut water and cooked sous vide for 1 hour at 65°.

About this Soju
Jinro, (pronounced Ji-low) soju has held its place as the number one Soju brand in Korea, since its launch in 1924 and is regarded as the number one selling spirit brand in the world.

Broke Artist Collective
Created by Tarik Evans

20ml	Jinro Soju (Unflavoured)
20ml	Five Farms Cream Liqueur
10ml	Gabriel Boudier Fig
50ml	Oat Milk
15ml	Monin Pistacho Syrup
1 Dash	20% Saline Solution
1/3	Pipette Vegan foamer

Glass:	Nic&Nora
Method:	Shake & Fine Strain
Ice:	None
Garnish:	Artist Card

Comments:
This drink was originally created for The Pineapple Club Birminghams 2022 Winter menu and was later adapted for this book.

About this Soju
Jinro, (pronounced Ji-low) soju has held its place as the number one Soju brand in Korea, since its launch in 1924 and is regarded as the number one selling spirit brand in the world.

For this drink Tarik draw four images, each of a different friend showcasing there passions and skills.

Simple Shochu/Awamori Terminology

The below are common terms we might see in the book or on a bottle. It's worth noting the Japanese language is extensive and many shochu/awamori words have secondary meanings or pronunciations. This list is in no way extensive but a good starting point:

Shochu Terminology:

Moromi (もろみ): Moromi is the fermented mash used to produce Shochu (and sake). It contains the ingredients, water, and koji, and it undergoes fermentation before distillation.

Koshu (古酒): Koshu refers to aged Shochu (and sake). The aging process can vary from a few month to several decades, resulting in a smoother and more complex spirit.

Kusu (古酒): Kusu is the Okinawa dialect for aged and is used to talk about aged Awamori, often aged for several years or more.

Shuzo (酒造): refers to a sake brewery or distillery in Japan. It is the place where sake, Shochu, Awamori, or other traditional alcoholic beverages are produced.

Bin (瓶): "bin" simply means "bottle."

Isshobin (升瓶): A traditional 1.8l bottle.

Honkaku (本格): "authentic" or "genuine."

Kuro (黒): Black

Ryukyu (琉球): Refers to the The Ryukyu Islands, a chain of islands in southern Japan, including Okinawa.

Ways to Enjoy Shochu

Here is a few ways which you can enjoy your Shochu:

Wari (Cut or Mixed with): "Wari" in this context, refers to the practice of blending alcohol with other liquids. You'll see this is then combine with other words to make specific drinks below.

Oyuwari: In Japanese, "Oyuwari" translates to "mixed with warm water." This is a traditional way of savouring Shochu, where the spirit is blended with warm water. The specific ratio of Shochu to water can vary, typically ranging from a 50/50 to a 60/40 ratio, allowing you to adjust the strength of the drink to your liking. The result is a warm and mellow Shochu beverage that can be particularly comforting, making it a popular choice during colder seasons or when seeking a more soothing Shochu experience.

Mizuwari: "Mizuwari" means "mixed with water" and is often served over ice. This method involves the dilution of Shochu with cold water, frequently poured over ice. Mizuwari creates a refreshing and chilled Shochu drink that's perfect for hot summer days. The addition of water helps bring out the nuanced flavours of the Shochu while keeping the beverage cool and enjoyable.

Sodawari: "Sodawari" refers to mixing Shochu with soda, often served over ice. By combining Shochu with soda water, you create a fizzy and effervescent Shochu drink. A modern way to enjoy Shochu which is now being adapted by many Shochu producers.

Cocktail: Shochu is a versatile spirit that can be used as a base in various cocktails. Whether you prefer it mixed with fruit juices, syrups, or other spirits, Shochu's adaptability allows you to create unique and flavourful cocktails.

Chūhai (Shochu-Highball): Chūhai is a Shochu-based highball, akin to a cocktail. This popular and refreshing way to enjoy Shochu involves mixing it with soda water and flavouring it with ingredients like citrus fruits or other flavourings. Chūhai is typically drank directly from cans or can be served over ice. More on these later.

Shochu/Awamori Drinking Vessels

Shochu vessels, much like sake, have been around for a long time, and each area has developed its own serving vessels. Below, I've written a brief description of the common drinking vessels you might see when visiting:

Sorakyu: A type of drinking vessel with a unique shape and design. Typically, it features a wide rim that tapers towards the bottom, resembling a gourd or calabash. This shape is not only aesthetically pleasing but also serves to enhance the aroma and flavour of the Shochu.

Gara & Choku: Traditional drinking sets typically seen in Kumamoto for rice Shochu. Traditionally, shochu in Hitoyoshi Kuma was strong, with 35 to 40% ABV. The preferred serving method was warmed. Gara refers to the larger pot with an elongated spout, which people heated over an open flame, which was then poured into a Choku, the smaller counterpart cup. They come in various designs and materials, adding to the overall aesthetic appeal of the sake-drinking experience.

Satsuma Kiriko: A type of cut glassware with intricate and beautiful patterns. It originated in the Satsuma region of Japan.

Dachibin: A traditional Okinawan drinking vessel that resembles a small jar or jug. It is commonly used to serve Awamori. Dachibin often features a distinctive shape and design, reflecting the rich cultural heritage of Okinawa.

Karakara: Legend states that an awamori-loving Buddhist monk created "karakara" in the image of a round rice cake. His ultimate goal was to make a jar that is hard to knock down, especially after drinking. There are two popular theories behind the vessel's name. Some believe the name came from the phrase asking to borrow it, "kase kase (let me borrow it)." Karakara features a marble that makes a distinctive "kara-kara" sound to let people know you're finished with your drink, so some people believe the name comes from this sound.

Ryukyu Glass: Glassware produced in the Ryukyu Islands of Japan, which includes Okinawa. These glasses often colourful (blue or red) and have intricate designs with relatively thicker glass than other glass cups. Ryukyu glass originated from the glass bottles left by American soldiers around Okinawa. People repurposed the discarded glass to make cups and other serving vessels. These are very common in Okinawa today.

Yushibin: A traditional Japanese drinking vessel, commonly used for serving and enjoying Awamori. It typically has a cylindrical shape and may vary in size.

Kuro Joka: A traditional shochu vessel originating in Kagoshima. Typically, a beautiful jet-black glaze and a distinct "flat kettle" shape. Slowly heating shochu over an open flame allows the shochu to open up.

Shochu Categories

Like sake, shochu is a complex category, primarily stemming from two factors: the complex and varied production processes and an extensive list of ingredients that can be used. The production of shochu can vary, and the type of distillation used results in different styles. There are many different styles, but I will mention three main ones below: Honkaku, Korui, and Konwa.

Honkaku Shochu

Honkaku shochu, often referred to as "authentic" or "single-distilled" shochu, is crafted with the utmost dedication to preserving the natural flavours of its primary ingredients. It is meticulously distilled once, allowing the essence of the base ingredient to shine through. This technique, rooted in tradition, results in a rich shochu experience, and showcases a deep appreciation of the source material's character. With approximately 55 permitted ingredients, including sweet potato, rice, and barley, Honkaku shoshu undergoes a koji-based multiple parallel fermentation, just like sake. Unlike shochu categories with added sugars or flavourings, Honkaku Shochu strictly forbids added sugar except for Kokuto Shochu from Amami (more on this later).

Legally, Honkaku Shochu must undergo only one distillation in a pot still, resulting in an ABV of 45% or less. Only ingredients from the specified list are allowed, meaning substances such as malt, fruit (except dates), juniper berries, and saccharine substances are prohibited. There are a few quirks in Japanese regulations meant to distinguish Honkaku Shochu from other alcohol categories. For example, colour is controlled, with spectrometer measurements kept under 0.08. This ensures that the liquid remains a lighter colour, preventing consumers from mistaking it for whisky. Additionally, the use of birch charcoal as a filter is not allowed, as this is commonly seen in vodka production.

Moving forward in this section of the book, all the Shochu we discuss will be Honkaku unless otherwise stated.

Korui Shochu
Korui shochu is a lighter and typically more neutral shochu. It is distilled multiple times, often with an emphasis on producing a smooth, milder, and neutral profile. The multiple distillations remove most (if not all) of the original base ingredient's character. Korui shochu is typically used as a neutral alcohol as the base for cocktails and other ready-to-drink products like canned Chuhai. It wouldn't be unfair to compare Korui shochu to vodka made around the world.

Konwa Shochu
Konwa shochu is made by blending different shochus (typically Korui and Otsurui) to achieve a balanced flavour. Distillers select various shochu bases, combining their unique qualities to create a distinct and well-rounded profile. Konwa shochu showcases the versatility of shochu, allowing for the creation of complex and enjoyable spirits.

Shochu Production

For production, I will be focusing solely on the Honkaku shochu process. Below is an overview of the main processes used for the production of Honkaku shochu; however, this doesn't include steps such as dilution, filtering, etc.

Just as in sake production, shochu production starts with koji. The primary ingredient, such as sweet potatoes, rice or barley, is first steamed or boiled to make it suitable for fermentation. The steamed base is then mixed with koji mould; the choice of koji is up to the brewery, but white koji is typically used. As with the koji process in sake, this is a crucial step that initiates the enzymatic conversion of starches into fermentable sugars. The type of koji-kin used and the duration of fermentation will influence the flavour and aroma of the final product. Rice koji is typically used for shochu production, but in shochu production koji can be made with rice, sweet potato, soba or barley. This being said, some styles, such as Iki shochu and Kokuto shochu, require rice koji to be used. When a blend of rice koji and another base ingredient is used on a shochu bottle, it will be expressed on the front in a percentage, looking something like '17% 米, 83% さつまいも' or in English '17% Rice, 83% Sweet Potato'.

One interesting note on Koji production is Yokka Koji. This koji is exclusively produced by a single distillery, Chuko, which is renowned for its clay pot tradition and innovative thinking. Finding information on Yokka Koji proved to be quite challenging, but when visiting the distillery and researching online this is the best way I can explain: "The koji-making process typically takes two days, but 'Yokka Koji' means 'four-

day koji'. Normal Awamori koji production results in the koji turning black when it sporulates, which apparently makes it less effective at breaking down the rice. However, with Yokka Koji, the resulting koji is not allowed to sporulate, therefore remaining pristine white! These techniques are laborious and require overnight monitoring". Chuko distillery in Okinawa who make a product called Yokka Koji Awamori. Yokka Koji Awamori is a rich mature yet much softer than you're average Awamori.

Production Process

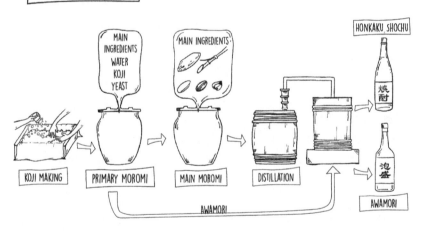

This graphic provides a concise overview of shochu production. Please note that it is a simplified guide and does not cover all the steps involved in detail.

Primary Moromi

Once your koji and base ingredient have been prepared, it's time to create the first moromi, sometimes called the starter. To make it, the koji, a portion of the base ingredient, water, and yeast are combined to create a mash. The first moromi establishes the foundation for a healthy yeast population, which is essential for the main fermentation's health.

Main Moromi

The first moromi is mixed with additional koji, water, base ingredients, and sometimes other ingredients, depending on the shochu type. This mixture is then allowed to ferment further in a larger vat. The second or main moromi is where the majority of alcohol production occurs. It is worth noting that this moromi is skipped in awamori production.

Distillation

In Honkaku shochu production, distillation is carried out in two ways: atmospheric or vacuum distillation. Typically, both of these methods are done in pot stills, with the latter being modified to create a vacuum. The goal here with both methods is the separation of alcohol from water and other components.

Distillation is a fundamental technique in the production of alcoholic spirits, and it serves to refine and concentrate the alcohol content of the liquid. In traditional Honkaku shochu production, a single distillation is the standard practice. This unique approach differs from many other spirit production methods found around the world. Both methods rely on the principle of heating the liquid to separate its components, but the resulting distillate will be worlds apart depending on the distillation pressure. Here's a closer look at both techniques:

Atmospheric Distillation
In atmospheric distillation, the fermented moromi is heated in pot stills at atmospheric pressure, which is the pressure found at sea level (approximately 1 atmosphere).

As the liquid is heated, the alcohol evaporates at a lower temperature than water, allowing for the separation of alcohol from the other components in the mash.

As the liquid is heated to "normal" distillation temperatures, this will preserve the unique flavours and aromas of the base ingredients but also allow for some cooking of these ingredients, releasing different compounds. Typically speaking, atmospheric distillates are more flavourful and robust compared to other distillation methods.

Vacuum Distillation
Vacuum distillation, on the other hand, is a process that occurs under reduced pressure.

Lowering the pressure lowers the boiling point of liquids. In vacuum distillation, this means that alcohol can be separated at lower temperatures than in atmospheric distillation. Vacuum distillation is used in the production of some spirits to minimise heat-related alterations to the flavour. This typically results in a lighter, more delicate distillate.

In Honkaku Shochu and Awamori production, the choice of atmospheric or vacuum distillation is significant. It emphasises the distiller's commitment to preserving the unique characteristics of the base ingredients and maintaining a pure and authentic expression of the spirit through multiple techniques. This, coupled with the single distillation requirement, demands a high level of expertise on the part of the distiller, as there is no opportunity to "hide" or correct issues arising from the fermentation process.

Bottling
Following distillation, shochu is usually aged for a brief period to mellow its flavours before it undergoes filtration and dilution to achieve the desired alcohol content. The choice of water used for dilution can also have an impact on the final taste.

Aging
Aging shochu is a process that enhances the characteristics of shochu, much like the aging process in Western-style spirits. While aging shochu in barrels isn't common, as most producers choose to keep their spirits unaged, some producers do opt to mature shochu in oak barrels or other suitable aging containers. This results in a gradual transformation of the shochu's flavour. Over time, it acquires subtle notes of vanilla, caramel, and spices, and its initial sharpness mellows. This aging process allows the different components of the spirit to harmonise, resulting in a smoother and more balanced spirit. In recent years, some producers have started to experiment with cask finishes, such as red wine or sherry barrels.

Kusu - Awamori
The Shitsugi aging method of Awamori is a distinctive and time-honoured technique used to mature Okinawan Awamori. Shitsugi, which translates to "continuous blending" in Japanese, is similar to the solera system used in sherry production. In this method, after bottling a portion of the

product, the older stock is replenished with younger stock to achieve a consistent and harmonious profile for a brewery's Awamori over time. By doing this year after year as the stock ages, distillers can balance the strengths and subtleties of each batch, resulting in a smoother and more well-rounded final product.

Ingredients

Shochu's versatility is indeed remarkable, as it can be made from an extensive list of ingredients, approximately totalling around 55. However, the precise count may vary slightly due to the common practice of grouping related ingredients together. For instance, "milk" and "powdered milk" are often listed as separate ingredients, even though they are closely related. As people categorising similar ingredients as one, this contributes to the variation in the count.

An extensive list is here:

Fruits and Vegetables
Leeks
Pumpkin
Tomato
Daikon Radish
Carrot
Onion
Bell Pepper
Green Pea
Green Onion
Lotus Root
Dates
Sweet Potato
Leeks

Fungi
Shiitake
Mushroom

Cereals
Barley
Rice
Buckwheat

Tea
Sencha
Matcha
Oolong

Seaweed
Nori
Tsunomata
Tsurutsuru
Kelp (Kombu)
Wakame

Nuts, Seeds, Beans	Herbs, Flowers, Trees
Sesame	Cactus
Chestnut	Yomogi (mugwort)
Peanut	Ashitaba
Acorn	Kuma Bamboo Grass
Stone Oak Acorn	Jiaogulan
Sunflower Seeds	Aloe
Japanese Horse Chestnut	Water Caltrop
Ume Plum Seeds	Asian Ginseng
Adzuki Bean	Safflower
Buckeye Seeds	Water Hyacinth
	Silver Vine
Other	Date Palm
Powder Milk	Saffron
Whey Powder	Lily Bulbs
Kudzu Flour	Fuki Flower
Milk	Sugar Cane
Sakekasu	Shiso (Perilla)

As you can probably guess, depending on the ingredients used, the resulting spirit will be very different. Generally speaking, you will have one of six ingredients as the base of your shochu: sweet potato, rice, sake lees, buckwheat, barley, or kokuto sugar. These ingredients provide enough sugars to convert into alcohol. After this, the remaining ingredients are typically used in conjunction with or in addition to the base, and these are sometimes referred to as aromatic ingredients. While this list might look extensive and exciting, some of these ingredients are seldom used anymore. For example, (to my knowledge) there are no producers making saffron shochu at the date of publication of this book. Others are in production but not being made on a mass scale. For example, ingredients like carrot and milk can be found in Japan at local stations to the distillery, but they are a rarity.

In the coming sections, I will discuss each main base in its own section and then discuss the aromatic styles together.

After each shochu style, I will explain why shochu is such a geographically influenced product. You see, while it can be produced anywhere in Japan, it is particularly favoured on the warmer islands, south of Japan's main island, Honshu.

Side note:
More detailed information on these geographical indicators is available from the National Tax Agency of Japan.

Imo Shochu (Sweet Potato) 芋焼酎

The first shochu to discuss is Imo Shochu. Predominantly from Kagoshima Prefecture, sweet potatoes were brought over from China, eventually making there way up the Ryūkyū island chain and finding a home in the volcanic soil of Kagoshima where rice and barley struggled to grow. Sweet potato shochu is the most popular shochu consumed in Japan. Classic imo shochu is renowned for its sweet and earthy flavours, which offer a rich umami driven, full-bodied taste with a hint of natural sweetness. However, with modern advancements in yeast developments we are seeing fruiter and more floral variants coming to market as well. One such shochu is Daiyame from Hamada Shuzo.

Hamada Shuzo was established in 1868, and is a shochu brewery located in the Kagoshima Prefecture. Daiyame is their traditional imo shochu, crafted from local sweet potatoes and black koji. This shochu offers pronounced aromas of lychee, a crisp palate with sweet undertones, and a refreshing fruit aftertaste. Very non-traditional.

While modern variants are much easier to mix, classic sweet potato shochu can be a difficult as it's rich umami profile can be challenging on the western pallet. However, I think that is exactly the quality which makes it an ideal canvas for innovative drinks.

Tickle me Ginger
Created by Klára Kopčiková

30ml	Hama No Imota Imo shochu
20ml	Cocchi Di Torino vermouth
20ml	Giffard Ginger syrup
2 Dash	Tonka Esprit

Glass:	Ceramic Sake Cup
Method:	Stirred
Ice:	Cubed
Garnish:	Nori

Comments:
This cocktail was made for *The Pineapple Clubs* Winter 2022 cocktail menu.

About this Shochu
The Chiyomusubi Brewery is situated in Tottori Prefecture and has been engaged in the production of sake and more recently, shochu, since 1865. This brewery places a particular focus on the use of locally sourced Goriki rice, an ancient rice variety that was nearly extinct until a revival effort in the 1980s breathed new life into it.

This is not a Lychee Martini
Created by Gento Torigata

30ml	Daiyame 40
15ml	London Dry gin
5ml	Merlet Peach liqueur
2.5ml	6% Malic Acid solution
10ml	2:1 Sugar syrup
1 Dash	Rose water

Glass:	Coup
Method:	Stirred
Ice:	None
Garnish:	Lime Coin (express over and float)

Comments:
The drink was originally made for customs requesting Lychee Martini's in London bar, which did not stock a lychee liqueur at the time.

About this Shochu
Hamada Shuzo was established in 1868 and is a shochu brewery located in the Kagoshima Prefecture. Daiyame is their traditional imo shochu, crafted from local sweet potatoes and black koji. This is the 40% international exclusive version of domestic 25% shochu that offers even more pronounced aromas of lychees and sweetness. At 40% ABV, it is also has a more noticeably alcoholic finish.

Eastern Wind
Created by Julian DeNéchauddeFéral

75ml	Imo Shochu
50ml	Pink grapefruit juice
25ml	Passionfruit pulp
25ml	Cinnamon honey
5ml	Fresh ginger juice

Glass:	Highball
Method:	Shake & Strain
Ice:	Cubed
Garnish:	Fresh cut dragonfruit

Comments:
Created in 2017 for Pan Asian concept rooftop bar of the legendary Oberoi Hotel in Delhi, with food provided by A. Wong.

Cinnamon Honey

20g	Cochin cinnamon stick
500ml	Acacia honey
250ml	Water

Break up cinnamon sticks and toast in a pan. Add water and mix well, strain and add 250ml of the hot cinnamon water to the honey and stir until dissolved. Let all ingredients cool down before fine straining through a muslin and bottling.

About this Shochu
Shochu Unknown

薩摩 Satsuma Shochu - Geographical Indicator
Kagoshima Prefecture
(excluding Amami City and Oshima District)
Designation Date: 22nd December 2005

Characteristics of liquor

"Satsuma", which is a pot distillation shochu, has the gorgeous, rich bouquet of the sweet potato from which it is made and is characterised by its sweet and rich taste which is in harmony with the bouquet created by using the high quality and fresh sweet potatoes grown in Kagoshima prefecture. Furthermore, it has a smooth palate from right after it is distilled.

Natural factor

The Shirasu Plateau which covers a large area of Kagoshima prefecture drains well and has many areas where the ground water level is low and is suitable for growing sweet potatoes. Therefore sweet potatoes have been grown here widely since the Edo period and it is Japan's biggest producer of sweet potatoes.

As a result, Kagoshima is a region well-suited to producing shochu from sweet potatoes as it can obtain a stable supply of this ingredient.

Human factor

The sweet potatoes were introduced from Ryukyu in the 17th century and as they were first grown in Satsuma, they became known as "Satsumaimo".

The "Satsuma" production technique has been established and passed on by the Kurose master brewers in the present-day Kurose district, Kasasacho, Minamisatsuma City, Kagoshima prefecture and Ata master brewers in the present-day Ata district, Kinpocho, Minamisatsuma city, Kagoshima prefecture.

Currently the Kagoshima Prefectural Institute of Industrial Technology takes the lead in technology development and dissemination as well as produces Kagoshima University's Shochu and Fermentation Science Education and Research Center also conducts research and development of shochu from sweet potatoes and nurtures human resources.

From the Meiji era on, the use of black koji mold (Aspergillus luchuensis) and white koji mold (Aspergillus kawachii), secondary fermentation process, development of apparatus for producing koji, and improvements to distillation apparatus, have allowed the production of even higher quality "Satsuma".

As a result of these improvements to production technology, the characteristics of the current "Satsuma" have been established.

Ingredients

The type of potato used is only sweet potato harvested in Kagoshima prefecture (excluding Amami city and Oshima district, hereinafter the same).

The koji used is only koji made from rice or from sweet potatoes harvested in Kagoshima prefecture.
Water collected in Kagoshima prefecture.

Production method

Fermentation of ingredients and distillation are performed in Kagoshima prefecture.

The moromi made of koji, sweet potatoes, and water is fermented and then distilled using a pot still.

If it is stored in the production process, storage is in Kagoshima prefecture.

The product is filled in Kagoshima prefecture in the containers that will be used to deliver the product to consumers

Kome Shochu (Rice) 米焼酎

Kome shochu is a distinguished spirit distilled from rice, which offers a refined and pristine profile. For me, Kome shochu embodies subtlety and sophistication. It is renowned for its exceptional lightness and carries within it gentle, almost ephemeral floral notes. Its nuanced character makes it an intriguing option for both sipping and as an ice-cold soda-wari (mixed with soda). The delicate nature of Kome shochu sets it apart from other Honkaku shochu. I like to think of Kome as a blank canvas upon which you, as mixologists, can paint flavour combinations.

Although most Kome shochu is inherently gentle, it does not shy away from making its presence known in a cocktail. Its slight floral undertones, reminiscent of blossoming flowers and fragrant perfume, infuse a layer of sophistication that elevates cocktails, albeit subtly. Its essence adds a charm that sets it apart from more common "flavourless" spirits, such as vodka. Typically, Kome shochu is vacuum distilled. This further adds to the light delicate nature of this shochu, which plays very well into the Japanese palate, which is often accustomed to milder and lighter flavours.

When mixing cocktails with Kome shochu, you can draw parallels to that of vodka-based cocktails. While I don't want you to see Kome as a vodka "replacement," Kome adds a dimension of sophistication with its gentle floral nuances. These delicate notes establish an aromatic quality not seen in vodka. For a modern bartender, this makes their cocktails more memorable and evocative.

Kome
Created by Klára Kopčiková

30ml	Hakutake Shiro shochu
10ml	Lychee liqueur
10ml	Yuzu sake
10ml	Cold Brewed jasmine tea syrup
Topped 60ml	Sparkling Nigori sake

Glass:	Kikichoko
Method:	Shake & Strain - Top with sake
Ice:	None
Garnish:	Edible flower

Comments:
Created in 2022 for a Shochu evening at Shibuya Underground bar in Birmingham.

Cold Brewed Jasmine Tea Syrup

10g	Loose leaf jasmine tea
1000ml	Water
1000g	Sugar

Add water and Loose leaf Jasmine together and cold brew until deserved flavour is achieved. After add sugar cold and stir until dissolved.

About this Shochu
Founded in 1900, Takahashi Shuzo has been focused on making authentic rice shochu in the Hitoyoshi Kuma region. Takahashi Shiro Shochu is a delicate, dry shochu. This is enhanced by vacuum distillation bringing out it's elegant aroma

and light taste, I would consider this a classic example of a Kome Shochu.

Natsu No Watermelon
Created by Maria Victoria Vecchione

45ml	Watermelon puree
25ml	Takara Kome shochu
25ml	Cointreau
10ml	Lime juice
10ml	1:1 Simple syrup
1	Fresh strawberry
1 Dash	Orange bitter

Glass:	Chilled martini glass
Method:	Shake & Strain
Ice:	None
Garnish:	Edible flower

Comments:
Muddle the strawberry with the lime juice. Add the rest of the ingredients and double strain into chilled martini glass.

About this Shochu
Takara Yokaichi Kome is a rice-based, single-distillation shochu. This process allows for greater complexity and more influences from the source material. Look for aromas of pear, jasmine rice, delicate white flowers, and rainwater. The palate is more savoury with flavours of salted pear, mineral, green olive, and lemon pith.

Kuma River Swizzle
Created by Chris Bostick

75ml	Hakutake Shiro shochu
15ml	Fresh grapefruit juice
15ml	Fresh lime juice
15ml	1:1 Simple syrup
1 Slice	Cucumber
1	Red grape

Glass:	Highball
Method:	Swizzle
Ice:	Crushed
Garnish:	Cucumber and Red Grape Flag

Comments:
Add all ingredients (except shochu) to a shaker and muddle. Add Shochu, shake with several pebbles of crushed ice. Pour into a highball glass. Top with more crushed ice and garnish with a cucumber and red grape flag

About this Shochu
Founded in 1900, Takahashi Shuzo has been focused on making authentic rice shochu in the Hitoyoshi Kuma region. Takahashi Shiro Shochu is a delicate, dry Shochu, this is helped by vacuum distillation bringing out it's elegant aroma and light taste, I would consider this a classic example of a Kome Shochu.

球磨 Kuma Shochu - Geographical Indicator
Kuma District and
Hitoyoshi City - Kumamoto Prefecture
Designation Date: 30th June 1995

Characteristics of liquor

"Kuma" which is a pot distillation shochu, usually has the mild sweet taste of rice and a refreshing flavour. Furthermore, products made with atmospheric distillation exude an aromatic bouquet characteristic of rice and those produced using reduced-pressure distillation exude a fruity bouquet.

Natural factor

Kuma district in Kumamoto Prefecture and Hitoyoshi city in the same prefecture are situated in the Kuma basin surrounded by mountains in the central area of Kyushu, and despite the low longitude, the average temperature in winter is low and the temperature variation is high. It has many days of heavy fog, and in such an environment fermentation at low temperatures and storage in a suitable environment are possible, making it a suitable area for production of shochu with a refreshing bouquet.

In addition, the water in the Kuma river system that flows through the Kuma basin is soft water suitable for shochu production, and "Kuma" retains the mild sweetness of rice through the use of water from this region.

Furthermore, the Kuma basin experiences high variations in temperature and is endowed with an abundant and high quality supply of water from the Kuma river, making it one of the leading areas for growing good quality rice in Kumamoto prefecture.

Human Factor

It is said that as the Kuma basin is blessed with abundant sources of water and plentiful rice production, the area has been able to keep producing shochu from rice since the era rice came to be valued. Furthermore, as it was an isolated region with the basin closed off deep in the mountains, rice was not subject to exploitation by outsiders. While in other regions production of shochu from rice was restricted due to famine and other reasons and people made liquor from ingredients other than rice, the brewers of Kuma were able to keep on producing shochu from rice.

The brewers of Kuma continued to be particular about using only rice as an ingredient in their shochu, and the current "Kuma" can be said to have its origin in such history, as the brewers pursued the flavour of Kuma and passed on their techniques.

As the rare visitors to the area were treated to "Kuma", it became known as "high quality liquor from a mysterious land".

Ingredients

The grains used is rice grown in Japan.
The koji rice used is only rice koji made from rice grown in Japan.
Water collected in Kuma district in Kumamoto prefecture or Hitoyoshi city in the same prefecture.

Production method

The fermentation of ingredients and distillation are performed in Kuma district, Kumamoto prefecture or Hitoyoshi city of the same prefecture.

It is made from moromi made by fermenting ingredients including rice, rice koji and water which is distilled in a pot still; provided however that this is limited to products where the primary moromi made from rice koji and water has rice koji and water added to it and is fermented further.

If it is stored in the production process, storage is in Kuma district, Kumamoto prefecture or Hitoyoshi city of the same prefecture.

The product is filled in Kuma district, Kumamoto prefecture or Hitoyoshi city in the same prefecture in the containers in which it will be delivered to consumers.

Kasutori Shochu (Sake Lees) 粕取り焼酎

Kasutori Shochu is a testament to the country's long-standing commitment to minimising waste and making the most of every ingredient. This shochu is derived from sake lees, the residual solids left behind after the sake brewing process. To make Kasutori shochu, you need to first start with the acquisition of sake lees. To obtain sake lees, sake brewers carefully press their fermented rice mashes, separating out the solids and the sake. The lees are a byproduct of brewing sake but are the precious raw material for Kasutori shochu.

Once the sake lees are gathered, the production of Kasutori shochu can commence. The process is fairly simple for most Kasutori (but can vary). Firstly, the lees are added to more water (and in some cases shochu) and then distilled to collect as much of the alcohol left over from the sake production as possible. This resulting liquid is then diluted and bottled. The remaining (very low alcohol) rice solids can be used as cattle feed or fertiliser by farmers, hence the waste minimisation aspect mentioned above.

Depending on the sake the lees came from, Kasutori shochu can possess distinct attributes. Typically, when drinking Kasutori shochu, you can expect to experience plenty of Ginjoka, the aromas typical of Ginjo grade sakes. Usually, it is fruity with apple and banana aroma esters. Some can be incredibly floral, like a daiginjo sake ramped up to 200%.

While Kasutori Shochu is a great shochu and a huge favourite of mine, many sake producers in Japan view this more as a waste management system than a labor of love. This makes finding Kasutori Shochu in the west less common. Typically, what I find here is from a brewery that has taken pride in their product. This viewpoint does have an upside, however, with Kasutori Shochu being made from a byproduct of sake production, it is often more affordable than other spirits, making it accessible and popular among local communities.

Kasutori Shochu is made all over Japan, meaning it has the weakest connection to a geographical location, therefore currently has no Geological Indicator.

All the cocktails in this section were design by Klára Kopčiková using Kimura Shuzo Daiginjo Kasutori Shochu

Founded in 1615 by the descendants of a distinguished samurai family, Kimura Shuzo remains unwavering in their commitment to age-old traditions. Their dedication to time-honoured artisanal techniques, pristine mountain spring water, and the highest quality premium rice, is emblematic of their enduring values. Located in the northern region of Akita Prefecture, under their esteemed Fukukomachi label, Kimura Shuzo crafts a range of multi-award-winning sake. This shochu stands as the sole distilled alcoholic beverage in their repertoire. This remarkable shochu is a vibrant floral and tropical bouquet reminiscent of watermelon and ripe cantaloupe, complemented by a velvety, smooth, and creamy texture that culminates in a refreshing, crisp, and dry finish.

Watermelon
Created by Klára Kopčiková

20ml	Kimura Shuzo Daiginjo Kasutori shochu
100ml	Fresh watermelon juice
5ml	Sugar
5 Dash	20% Saline solution

Glass:	Square Highball
Method:	Build And Stir
Ice:	Block ice
Garnish:	Watermelon ball

Comments:
Created in 2022 for a drinks only tasting menu at Shibuya Underground bar in Birmingham. Watermelon might look simple in its creation but this drink was designed to allow the Kasutori shochu to stand front and centre.

Anime
Created by Klára Kopčiková & Samuel Boulton

20ml	Kimura Shuzo Daiginjo Kasutori shochu
15ml	Gabriel Boudier Lychee liqueur
10ml	Muyu Jasmine Verte
5ml	Gabriel Boudier Blue curacao liqueur
20ml	Acid mix
100ml	Lemonade

Glass:	Highball
Method:	Build And Stir
Ice:	Cubed

Garnish: Pokemon Card

Comments:
Created in Winter 2022 for a drinks only tasting menu at
Shibuya Underground bar in Birmingham. Anime pays homage
to the rise of anime culture in Japan, this drink is a modern take
on a Chuhai. A classic drink consumed while playing video
games in Japan.

Acid Mix
94g   Filtered Water
4g   Citric Acid Powder
2g   Malic Acid Powder

Place everything in a container and stir until acids are
dissolved.

So Fresh and So Clean
Created by Klára Kopčiková

40ml   Kimura Shuzo Daiginjo Kasutori Shochu
15ml   Grapefruit Juice
10ml   Lime Juice
20ml   Grapefruit and Pink Pepper 'Oleo'
Top   3 Cents Bergamot and Mandarin Soda

Glass: Wine Glass
Method: Build And Stir
Ice: Cubed
Garnish: Grapefruit Zest Discarded

Comments:
This drink was created by Klára Kopčiková for this book.

Grapefruit and Pink Pepper 'Oleo'
1	Grapefruit Juiced
35g	Crushed pink pepper corns
500g	60:40 Sugar Syrup

Juice the grapefruit and reserve the remaining zest. Set the grapefruit juice aside. Combine the zest with 35g of crushed pink peppercorns and 500g of 60:40 sugar syrup. Sous vide the mixture at 65 degrees for 5 hours, then strain and bottle it.

Mugi Shochu (Barley) 麦焼酎

Barley started to be used to make alcohol in Japan as rice (the domestically preferred crop) seemed too valuable and needed to be reserved for tax purposes (more on this later when talking about Ike Island's Geological Indicator). Barley is a versatile cereal grain with many varieties around the world. In Mugi shochu production, there are two main varieties: two-row barley and six-row barley. These refer to the number of rows of kernels on the barley stalk. Two-row barley, as the name suggests, has two rows of kernels per stalk, while six-row barley has six rows.

Two-row barley is preferred for making Mugi shochu primarily because it thrives in cooler climates. This makes it well-suited for cultivation in regions with colder winters and milder summers, such as certain parts of Japan (although most barley is currently imported). Two-row barley kernels tend to be larger compared to six-row barley. These larger kernels contain a higher starch content and lower protein amounts, which are desirable for Honkaku Shochu production. Much like rice used in sake production, barley for Mugi shochu is also polished. It is typically polished to around 60-65% of its original size. This process is essential for refining the grain ensuring that only the best-quality parts of the barley is used.

Mugi shochu is sometimes likened to whisky due to the use of barley as a primary ingredient. However, it is important to note that Mugi shochu has its own unique character, which vastly distinguishes it from whisky. Mugi shochu, in comparison, is very light and mellow. The lower ABV and typical vacuum distillation differentiates Mugi Shochu from the high esters and robust profile typically found in whiskey. Another reason for this is that all whiskey is made to be aged (with the exclusion of some white dogs, etc.), while Mugi can be unaged; thus, this means the product needs to be mellow and ready to drink soon after production.

Mugi
Created by Klára Kopčiková

35ml	Ginza No Suzume Shirokoji Mugi shochu
10ml	Yellow chartreuse
15ml	Rinquinquin
15ml	Vanilla syrup
20ml	Lemon juice
1/3 pipette	Foamer

Glass:	Nick & Nora
Method:	Shake & Strain
Ice:	None
Garnish:	Lemon Twist

Comments:
Created in 2022 for a Shochu evening at Shibuya Underground bar in Birmingham.

About this Shochu
Ginza No Suzume Shirokoji Mugi Shochu from Oita Prefecture on Kyushu Island, Yatsushika Brewery offers a classic barley shochu. Crafted from barley Koji with white koji-kin, it's a light, mild, and refreshing introduction to the category.

Wabi-Sabi
Created by Hyppolite Civins

50ml	Aokage Mugi Shochu
15ml	Monin White Penja Pepper Cordial
60ml	Akashi Tai Umeshu Soda
2 Dash	Chocolate Bitters

Glass:	Ceramique Tribeca Malt
Method:	Build, lightly stir while topping up
Ice:	Block Ice
Garnish:	Dried Raspberry Rim

Comments:
Wabi-Sabi is the Japanese concept that teach us to celebrate imperfection, Hyppolite, believe the art of creating drinks is developing a lot of imbalanced cocktails and making mistakes in order to reach the sweet harmony of your final presentation. This drink was created for The Great Honkaku Shochu & Awamori contest of UKBG 2023.

Akashi-Tai Umeshu Soda

250ml	Akashi-Tai Umeshu Sake
250ml	Filtered water
2g	Malic acid
1g	Salt

Carbonate and keep cold.

About this Shochu
Aokage Mugi is crafted using 100% Two-Row Barley sourced from Kyushu island. Using Kagoshima Yeast No.2 and Barley

as the Koji Base, then utilises white Koji-Kin. Distillation is achieved through a Direct-Injection Steam Pot Still - Atmospheric method under the guidance of Tadashi Yanagita.

The water component is equally exceptional, sourced from the pristine springs of the Kirishima Mountains within the Miyazaki Prefecture. Production is a deliberately slow fermentation at low temperatures before distillation. During the distillation phase, Yanagita-san uses a precise heat manipulation technique, effectively "toasting" the liquid as it circulates, yielding distinct roasty undertones.

After distillation, the spirit undergoes an aging process in glass tanks. It is then hand filtered, using custom-made horsehair strainers to carefully strain the upper layers of the tanks. This painstaking process serves to eliminate impurities while preserving the essential oils and flavours that contribute to the spirit's unique and distinguished character.

Town
Created by Klára Kopčiková

30ml	Ginza No Suzume Shirokoji Mugi shochu
10ml	Nardini Grappa 40
10ml	Frangelico
10ml	Vanilla syrup
2 Dash	Angostura bitters

Glass:	Nick & Nora
Method:	Shake & Strain
Ice:	None
Garnish:	Lemon twist

Comments:
This drink was apart of a 5 course drinks only tasting event and was never design to be drank alone. The event was themed around the Studio Ghibli film, Princess Mononoke. Prince Ashitaka arrives to Iron Town, a highly industrial city. The drink is inspired by the human society

About this Shochu
Ginza No Suzume Shirokoji Mugi Shochu from Oita Prefecture on Kyushu Island, Yatsushika Brewery offers a classic barley shochu. Crafted from barley Koji with white koji-kin, it's a light, mild, and refreshing introduction to the category.

壱岐 Iki Shochu - Geographical Indicator
Iki City - Nagasaki Prefecture
Designation Date: 30th June 1995

Characteristics of liquor

"Iki", which is a Pot distillation shochu, retains the fresh bouquet of barley from which it is made and the sweet and deep flavour of rice koji. It has a sharp taste originating from the water of the region.

Natural Factors

Iki City, Nagasaki Prefecture, is an archipelago centering on Ikinoshima island which is in the Genkainada Sea north of Kyushu, and the region has a rich supply of underground water which has been refined by the basaltic layer over a long period of time.

Iki's underground water, which is rich in minerals and pure, is one of the important ingredients in Iki, and is used in many ways from ingredient preparation to mixing the distilled unprocessed shochu ("Genshu") with water. In the production process, the underground water of Iki maintains good fermentation and gives Iki its deep flavour, as well as eliciting a sharp taste due to the use of the underground water for mixing with the Genshu.

Human factors

It is said that the production of "Iki" began as local farmers produced it for their own consumption due to the wealth of groundwater in Iki and the abundance of rice and barley harvests.

The roots of Pot distillation shochu lie in the production of distilled liquor on the Chinese continent and in south-east Asia which was subsequently introduced in Japan. According to the "Korean Peninsula Route theory" which is one of the influential theories espousing this route, Japan and Korea were actively engaged in trade in the 15th century, at which time Korea was already manufacturing distilled liquor. This technology was introduced to Japan via Tsushima and Iki, and it is presumed that the origins of production of shochu lie in this era.

Furthermore, historical records show that Iki, Nagasaki was the earliest region in Japan to introduce production of shochu made from barley and it is assumed to be the "birthplace of barley shochu".

Barley shochu produced in other regions is produced from barley koji and barley, however, "Iki" is traditionally produced from rice koji and barley, using a ratio of 1:2, and this traditional method is one of the factors in establishing the characteristics of "Iki".

Ingredients
Grains use only barley.
Only rice koji produced from rice is used.
The weight ratio of rice koji and grains for the moromi must be approximately 1:2.
Water collected in Iki city in Nagasaki prefecture.

Production method
The product is made by fermenting rice koji and water to make the primary moromi, to which is added steamed grains and

water before fermenting further to make the secondary moromi, which is distilled in a pot still.

Fermenting and distillation of the ingredients is performed in Iki city, Nagasaki prefecture.

If the product is stored in the production process, it is stored in Iki city, Nagasaki prefecture.

The product is bottled in Iki city Nagasaki prefecture in the containers it's final container

Kokuto Shochu (Kokuto Sugar) 黒糖焼酎

Kokuto shochu comes from the picturesque Amami Islands, nestled in the southern part of Japan. These islands, part of the Ryukyu Archipelago, have a rich history and cultural heritage, significantly influencing the production of Kokuto sugar.

The Amami Islands have been inhabited for thousands of years, and their culture has been shaped by interactions with various Asian cultures. One of the most distinctive aspects of Amami's history is its sugarcane cultivation, dating back to the 17th century when sugarcane was introduced to the islands. This historical connection with sugarcane forms the foundation of Kokuto shochu's key ingredient - Kokuto sugar.

Kokuto sugar, used in the production of this unique shochu, is a type of unrefined brown sugar made from the juice of sugarcane. The sugar-making process in Amami has a long history, traditionally produced using wooden tools and left to slowly crystallise. This method imparts a rich licorice-like complexity to the sugar, which carries over into the final shochu.

Kokuto sugar is so highly regarded in Japan that simply reducing it to 'brown sugar' would be a disservice to the quality and history of the sugar.

What makes Kokuto shochu a shochu is its mandatory inclusion of rice koji in the production process. The rice koji plays a vital role in breaking down compounds in the sugar, while yeast is converting them into alcohol.

While the idea of Kokuto shochu might evoke thoughts of rum due to the use of sugar, the similarities aren't as strong as you might believe. Kokuto shochu tends to be much milder and lighter compared to rum. However, it does retain a characteristic fruity note. This fruity note, combined with the complex profile, creates a well-balanced and nuanced spirit.

Shochu Pornstar
Created by Samuel Boulton

25ml	Lento Kokuto shochu
25ml	PStar liqueur
100ml	PStar mix

Glass:	Coup
Method:	Shake & Fine Strain
Ice:	None
Garnish:	Shot Akashi Tai Sparkling Sake & half a Passionfruit

Comments:

PStar mix

10ml	Passionfruit puree
50ml	Passionfruit juice
15ml	Vanilla syrup
5ml	Lime juice

No cocktail menu would be complete without Douglas Ankrah, the inventor of the Pornstar Martini. Douglas was a personal friend of mine and passed away days before a planned weekend of Pornstar events together. Douglas began his career at London's Hard Rock Café before establishing LAB, the London Academy of Bartending, in the Atlantic Bar in 1996. Three years later, he co-founded the LAB Bar in Soho, which quickly became an industry hub and a training ground for leading bartenders. The success of this venture led Douglas to open Townhouse in 2002. Over its eight-year existence, this Knightsbridge bar, renowned for its 80-strong cocktail list, earned a place on many 'best bars in the world' lists. This drink is a simple shochu take on his famous cocktail. To the uninitiated, there wouldn't be much difference, but the inclusion of Shochu rounds out the acidic nature of passionfruit and adds a touch of complexity.

About this Shochu:
Lento, a popular Kokuto shochu brand from the Amami island, is an excellent choice for beginners looking to explore this unique style of shochu. Comprising 68% Kokuto sugar and 32% rice koji, and made with white koji-kin, Lento undergoes a single vacuum distillation process using pot stills. Despite its light and mellow flavour profile, Lento offers a natural and well-balanced taste, making it a smooth and enjoyable choice for those new to Kokuto Shochu.

Lento Chuhai
Created by Alexander Taylor

50ml	Lento Kokuto shochu
10ml	Spanish white vermouth
10ml	Falernum
1 Dash	Peach bitters
75ml	Top soda

Glass:	Highball
Method:	Build and Stir
Ice:	Cubed
Garnish:	Grapefruit zest

Comments:
A beautiful modern take on a classic Chuhai.

About this Shochu:
Lento, a popular Kokuto shochu brand from the Amami island, is an excellent choice for beginners looking to explore this unique style of shochu. Comprising 68% Kokuto sugar and 32% rice koji, and made with white koji-kin, Lento undergoes a single vacuum distillation process using pot stills. Despite its light and mellow flavour profile, Lento offers a natural and well-balanced taste, making it a smooth and enjoyable choice for those new to Kokuto Shochu.

Run-DMC
Created by Samuel Boulton

25ml	Hama-Chidori-no-Uta Undiluted Kokuto shochu
20ml	Green chartreuse
25ml	Monin kiwi syrup
20ml	ODK lime juice
1/3 pipette	Vegan foamer
3 Dash	Yuzu bitters
3 Dash	20% Saline solution
20ml	Top appletiser

Glass:	Nick & Nora
Method:	Shake & fine strain
Ice:	None
Garnish:	White chocolate shard

Comments:
This drink was originally created for The Pineapple Club Birminghams 2022 Winter menu and was later adapted for this book.

About this Shochu:
A fantastic shochu, with its 38% ABV leaves you really feeling the full Kokuto flavour! Using only brown sugar produced in Amami Oshima as its main ingredient, it is then atmospheric distilled and left at 38%, and finally aged for 7 years.

Regional Collective Trademark
Kokuto - Shochu
Amami Islands - Kagoshima Prefecture
Designation Date: 6th February 2009

Amami brown sugar shochu earned permission for production only in the Amami Islands with the use of rice koji and brown sugar as base ingredients.

The Amami archipelago sits approximately halfway between Kagoshima and Okinawa. It contains eight islands, including Amami Oshima. The total population of the archipelago is about 120,000. It covers a total area of around1,231 km², all considered part of Kagoshima prefecture.

Amami Oshima, the largest island, spans an area of 712.39 km², sitting about 370 km from mainland Kagoshima. There are many flat farmlands in the north, mostly used for sugarcane cultivation, while most of the south is mountainous. While influenced by both the mainland Kagoshima and Okinawa, the area has its own distinct culture. These customs include their own island songs, unique textiles, and brown sugar shochu. Amami islands are the only place in Japan that is legally permitted to produce brown sugar shochu.

The Amami Islands boast abundant natural beauty. Highlights include the largest subtropical laurel forest in Japan and the coral reefs in the Sea of Amami. In addition, millions of years of isolation fostered unique biodiversity in the area, housing many of the world's rarest creatures.

Local Ingredients

The Amami Islands enjoy suitable conditions for growing various crops due to the warm temperature and heavy rainfall. However, these crops face potential damage from abundant pests and typhoons as well.

Over 99% of the cultivated land is farmland dedicated to producing sugar cane, vegetables, flowers, livestock, fruit trees, and more. Half of the active farming area produces sugar cane.

Conventional wisdom states that the first brown sugar came to Japan from a Chinese Buddhist monk over 1200 years ago. Several theories speculate how sugarcane cultivation and the sugar manufacturing method arrived in the islands. The most popular theory proposes a 17th century dispatch to the Ryukyu Kingdom learned the technique and brought it back.

Subsequently, the technique spread to the other islands in the archipelago. Later, the ruling Shimazu clan encouraged brown sugar production, making it the main product of Amami.

Soba Shochu (Buckwheat) 蕎麦焼酎

Soba Shochu, a Japanese distilled spirit with a rich history, offers a unique and distinct profile yet again. This exceptional shochu first made its appearance in the Miyazaki Prefecture in 1973, thanks to the pioneering efforts of Unkai Shuzo, who were instrumental in introducing Soba shochu to the world. This means Soba shochu has only been around for 50 years (at the time of this book's publication).

One of the notable challenges in producing Soba shochu is the nature of buckwheat itself. Buckwheat presents some difficulties during the production process. Unlike some other grains, buckwheat needs to be dehisced, or have its hard outer hull removed, before it can be ground and fermented. This extra step adds to the labour and time involved in crafting Soba Shochu but is essential for unlocking the rich flavour within buckwheat.

Another challenge of producing Soba shochu is its struggle with moisture retention, which poses challenges in the Koji and fermentation process. To address this, traditional Soba shochu production once involved the use of other Koji, such as rice or barley, to help maintain the necessary moisture levels. This blending of grains allowed for a smoother fermentation process and a more predictable production process.

However, with the advancements in scientific understanding and production techniques, the industry has made remarkable strides. Today, it is possible to produce Soba shochu with 100% buckwheat. Generally speaking, Soba Shochu has a distinct nutty and earthy quality; even at 25% ABV, it's not a spirit that will easily disappear in a cocktail.

While Soba Shochu is mainly confined to production on Kyushu Island, like Kasutori it's lack of connection to on distinct geographical location, means it is unlikely to be granted a Geological Indicator.

All the below cocktail in this section are using Towari Soba, produced by Takara Shuzo, which exclusively uses 100% buckwheat, setting it apart from the more traditional soba shochu varieties that rely on ingredients like rice or barley koji.

This distinctiveness truly shines through in its profile, offering a nutty essence complemented by a subtle smokiness reminiscent of Scottish single malts. Distilled under standard pressure to unlock rich and robust profile.

Hara-Kiri
Created by Klára Kopčiková & Samuel Boulton

25ml	Takara Soba Towari shochu
20ml	Gabriel Boudier crème de cacao blanc
15ml	Tempus Fugit anana liqueur

Glass:	Nick & Nora
Method:	Stirred
Ice:	None
Garnish:	Dark chocolate shard

Comments:
This drink was part of a 6 course drinks only tasting menu at Shibuya Underground, Birmingham UK. Inspired by Seppuku, also called hara-kiri, a form of Japanese ritualistic suicide by disembowelment. While harakiri refers to the act of disemboweling oneself, seppuku refers to the ritual and usually would involve decapitation after the act as a sign of mercy. The drink was sweet and sharp to signify harakiri's sweet release of death.

Cold Noodles
Created by Robert Wood

30ml	Takara Soba Towari shochu
15ml	Nikka Coffey gin
15ml	Dolin Vermouth de chambery blanc
10ml	Sūpāsawā
25ml	Sudachi cordial
1ml	Sudachi Kombu ponzu
1ml	The Japanese bitters umami

20ml   Sobacha

Glass: Nude Pony
Method: Pre batched 120ml per Portion
Ice: None
Garnish: Toasted Sesame Oil

Comments:

A Gimlet style cocktail based on a variety of Summer cold noodle dishes from across Asia, packing umami flavours alongside citrus freshness.

Sudachi Cordial

150ml	Sudachi Puree (100%)
350ml	Cane Syrup 1:1
10g	Citric Acid
5g	Malic Acid
1g	Maldon Sea Salt

Add acids and salt to Sudachi, stir and allow to disperse. Add syrup and stir again. Store in plastic bottle.

Sobacha

| 200ml | Filtered Water |
| 5g | Roasted Buckwheat Tea (Memil-cha) |

Brew grains with water at 95c for 10 minutes. Pass through 100u Superbag and store in plastic bottle.

Banana Blaise
Created by Blaise Bachelier

40ml	Takara Soba Towari Shochu
20ml	Giffard Banane du Bresil
10ml	Brown Cacao Liqueur
25ml	Cream

Glass:	Nick & Nora
Method:	Double Shake & Fine Strain
Ice:	None
Garnish:	Grated Nutmeg

Comments:
This drink was created for this book and was inspired by a White Russian.

Awamori 泡盛

Awamori is again a unique in shochu production. However, it holds a special place in the hearts of the people of Okinawa. This regional specialty has a rich history and distinct characteristics tied to the island of Okinawa. To truly appreciate Awamori, it's essential to understand its origins, production process, and the unique qualities that separate it from other spirits in Japan.

The Japanese law distinguish Awamori as a subcategory of shochu, however I think this is rudimentary and more a bureaucratic system. Awamori follows a slightly different production process and has a big change in the ingredients required. For me while it is a shochu by classification, Awamori is a very different spirit both in taste and history.

Okinawa is a picturesque island in southern Japan with a rich cultural heritage influenced by both Japanese and regional indigenous traditions. It's known for its stunning natural beauty, vibrant festivals, and, of course, its unique alcoholic beverage, Awamori. The history of Awamori on the island dates back centuries, making it an integral part of Okinawa's cultural identity.

The history of distillation in Okinawa is fascinating and closely linked to the island's historical ties with trade and cultural exchange. Distillation techniques likely reached Okinawa through trade connections with China and Southeast Asia. This exchange introduced the concept of distillation to the island, laying the foundation for the creation of Awamori.

While Awamori can technically be produced anywhere in Japan, most of it is associated with Okinawa. It is essential to note that there is a specific distinction between "Awamori" and "Ryukyu Awamori." Awamori produced in Okinawa, also known as Ryukyu Awamori, must adhere to certain criteria, including the use of Thai rice, which sets it apart from Awamori produced in other regions of Japan.

Thai rice, is a strain of Indica rice, (more typically known as long grain rice). While sake and most table rice in Japan is a strain of Japonica (characterised by being shorter, rounder, think of risotto rice).

Awamori's most notable attribute is the intense flavour which is much stronger than any other shochu. It is regularly seen at a higher ABV, and uses 100% black koji which adds to its robust, fragrant aroma. When sipping Awamori, one can expect a strong, rich spirit with hints of tropical fruit notes, creating a unique and unforgettable drinking experience.

Prince
Created by Klára Kopčiková

40ml	Harusame Kari awamori
15ml	Matcha cordial
10ml	Raspberry syrup
15ml	Lemon juice
Top	Tonic

Glass:	Highball
Method:	Shake & Strain
Ice:	Cubed
Garnish:	Printed card a garnish

Comments:
This drink was apart of a 5 course drinks only tasting event and was never design to be drank alone. The event was themed around the Studio Ghibli film, Princess Mononoke. Prince Ashitaka, who we meet right at the begging of the film, is a kind and strong character, devoted to his village, this drink is bright (thanks to the raspberry and matcha) just like his personality, with a bitter edge of tonic, symbolising his fighting abilities. On the card, there's one of his people, a girl from the Emishi village.

Matcha Cordial
2g	Matcha
1g	Tartaric Acid
0.25g	Citric Acid
0.15g	Malic Acid
100g	Boiling Water
85g	Sugar

Method:

Mix all ingredients until everything has fully combined. Then pass them through a wet coffee filter. It is crucial that the filter is wet, or you'll lose some yield, and the flavour will be altered. After 30 seconds of filtration, take what has already come through and refilter; this will help ensure that the final product is perfectly clear, as the initial 30 seconds of filtering can still yield a slightly hazy result.

About this Awamori

Established in 1946, Miyazato Distillery emerged shortly after the conclusion of World War II, nestled on the tropical Naha island within Japan's Okinawa Prefecture. Harusame Kari offers an aromatic spirit brimming with nutty nuances, with hazelnut and walnut notes, complemented by undertones of cream, fudge, vanilla, black pepper, and delicate florals.

Man'naka
Created by Hyppolite Civins

60ml	Harusame Kari awamori
35ml	Black Procini cordial

Glass: Goblet
Method: Thrown
Ice: None
Garnish: Awamori & Yuzushu foam

Comments:
Man'naka means 'midway': 'If something is midway between two places, it is in between them and at the same distance from each of them.' This concept represents the layers in the drinks and is inspired by the spirit, symbolising 'less is more' and relaxation.

Black Procini Cordial
100ml	Water
50g	Sugar
50g	Procini Mushrooms
7g	Citric Acid
	Activated Charcoal

Infused water, sugar and mushrooms sous vide until desired flavour, strain out solids and add active charcoal and acid.

About this Awamori
Established in 1946, Miyazato Distillery emerged shortly after the conclusion of World War II, nestled on the tropical Naha

island within Japan's Okinawa Prefecture. Harusame Kari offers an aromatic spirit brimming with nutty nuances, with hazelnut and walnut notes, complemented by undertones of cream, fudge, vanilla, black pepper, and delicate florals.

The Breath Before
Created by Thomas Ryan-Tarrant

60ml	Harusame Kari awamori
15ml	Genmaicha infused Stones ginger wine
2 Dash	Ms Betters Mt Fuji bitters

Glass:	Rocks
Method:	Thrown
Ice:	Cubed
Garnish:	Expressed and Discarded Lime Peel & Pickled Ginger

Comments:
Inspired by the concept of Ma, which Thomas encountered while studying Aikibujutsu and Shinkendo. The art of distancing yourself from your opponent while avoiding vulnerability.

With this idea in mind, you can set out to craft a straightforward yet impactful drink. The goal was to create a beverage that will evoke the essence of a Dark n Stormy, utilising Awamori to infuse it with the distinctive acidity and body of black koji.

About this Awamori

Established in 1946, Miyazato Distillery emerged shortly after the conclusion of World War II, nestled on the tropical Naha island within Japan's Okinawa prefecture.

Harusame Kari offers an aromatic spirit brimming with nutty nuances, with hazelnut and walnut notes, complemented by undertones of cream, fudge, vanilla, black pepper, and delicate florals.

Victoria's Vesper
Created by Victoria Vera

30ml	Yokka Koji Awamori
30ml	Roku Japanese Gin
15ml	Oka Brand Yuzu Liqueur
1 Drop	The Japanese Bitters Umami Bitters

Glass:	Chilled Martini or Coupe
Method:	Stirred
Ice:	None
Garnish:	Cocktail onion

Comments: In a world where everything is new and everyone is trying to reinvent the wheel, Victoria, finds comfort in the classics. At her Shochu Bar - Tsunami Panhandle, Victoria takes classic cocktails and adds a Japanese twist. Victoria says "Yokka Koji is a phenomenal Genshu Awamori, with earthy, somewhat mushroom-like quality that adds complexity to this martini that vodka would not. The umami bitters complement this Awamori and builds on the savoury notes. One of the predominant botanicals in Roku gin is Yuzu peel, which enhances the Yuzu Liqueur, which replaces the traditional Lillet Blanc. The sweet tartness of the yuzu really balances well with the umami elements, creating a refreshing martini. The onion garnish complements this savoury cocktail."

About this Awamori: Yokka Koji Awamori from Chuko distillery on Naha Island of Okinawa. Yokka Koji alongside the umami qualities has hints of pear, green apple and rose with a rich body, a smooth, luxurious texture and a long, involved finish.

琉球 Ryukyu Awamori - Geographical Indicator
Okinawa
Designation Date: 30th June 1995

Characteristics of liquor

"Ryukyu," which is a pot still distilled liquor made by distillation of fermented mash made from rice koji using the black koji mould and water as ingredients, has a robust flavour from the optimal amount of oil originating from the rice koji used as an ingredient. Products made from the traditional atmospheric distillation have a pleasant aroma, while products made from reduced-pressure distillation have the flavour of fruits such as apples and bananas. In particular, aged liquors (stored three years or longer) made from atmospheric-distillation have a rich and deep aroma, a harmony of a sweet vanilla aroma from the components from the rice broken down by the enzymes from the black koji mould and the aroma of Matsutake mushrooms.

Microbiological factor

The academic name for the black koji mould (Aspergillus luchuensis) used in "Ryukyu" is a name originating in Ryukyu, and specified as a National Fungi.

"Ryukyu" uses only rice koji made using black koji mould, and water and yeast are added to the rice koji and fermented, with the whole koji preparation being a traditional production technique unique to Ryukyu and passed down through generations in Okinawa prefecture. It is this technique that gives "Ryukyu" its sensory elements, including a rich and deep aroma and robust flavour.

Natural factor

Okinawa prefecture is in the Ryukyu Islands to the south-west of the Japanese archipelago and has been an important trading port in East Asia since old times. With its subtropical climate come high temperatures, high humidity and significant rainfall. In sake brewing in such climate, the possibility of spoiling due to unwanted bacteria in the fermentation of moromi is high. However, the black koji mould which forms a high amount of citric acid compared to other koji moulds maintains good fermentation, and the various components formed by this black koji mould give "Ryukyu" its unique characteristics.

In addition, the Ryukyu limestone belt runs through Okinawa, and the water is hard water with abundant mineral content, and as the climate is hot, the microorganisms (black koji mould and yeast) are active, creating a complex and rich flavour.

Human factor

The history of production of "Ryukyu" is long and there are several theories about the history of the production techniques. Because there are similarities with the production methods of distilled liquors used by the trading partners of the Ryukyu kingdom, it is said that various techniques were introduced over 500 years ago from South-east Asia or the Chinese continent through cultural exchange which conformed to the weather and culture of Ryukyu are the origin for Ryukyu's unique traditional production method.

"Ryukyu" is also called as "Ryukyu Awamori" or "Awamori." There are many different theories about the origin of these names. Some say that the name, "Awamori(literally, bubbles that rise and swell)," which has an alcoholic percentage of over 40% immediately after distillation, came from the way bubbles are formed in a container when the liquor is poured from a height to measure the alcoholic content. Awamori with a particularly high alcohol percentage is also called, "Hanazake" (literally, flower sake), since the bubbles in the container are layered, looking like as if flowers are in full bloom.

"Ryukyu" has a culture of being matured after distillation over the years. Ryukyu that has been aged for at least three years is called, "kusu (aged shochu)." Whisky or other liquors are generally stored in barrels and matured as they obtain the fragrance component of barrels. "Ryukyu," on the other hand, is stored in jars and bottles and matured as the flavour component contained in the sake itself goes through physical and chemical changes. Thus, Ryukyu is characterised by its ongoing maturity even after being packed in a container and put on the market. At the geographical origin, the culture and techniques of nurturing "Ryukyu" into "kusu" by consumers by themselves, called "shitsugi" (sake making) has been established.

Ingredients

Only rice koji made using the black koji mould belonging to Aspergillus luchuensis is used for the rice koji.

Water collected in Okinawa prefecture is used for the water.

Production method

Fermentation of ingredients and distillation is performed in Okinawa prefecture.

Moromi made by fermenting the ingredients of rice koji and water is distilled in a pot still.

If it is stored in the production process, storage is in Okinawa prefecture.

The product is filled in Okinawa prefecture in the containers in which it will be delivered to consumers.

Other Awamori Based Alcohols

While it's great to delve into the rich history of Okinawa and Awamori, Okinawa is also moving with modern times, much like shochu, which serves as the base for other products such as Chuhai, Umeshu, and as the added alcohol in some sake. Producers in Okinawa have more recently begun using Awamori as the base for other beverages. At the time of this publication, there are three producers in Okinawa making Gin with Awamori as the base. These gins are particularly intriguing to a European like myself, as they don't need to adhere strictly to the dominant flavour of Juniper.

During my time in Okinawa, I tried a few gins, all of which were unmistakably gin, but with a distinct local take, featuring local citrus and botanicals that were very foreign to my Western palate.

Another fascinating product I encountered was called 'Sake X Awamori,' where Awamori was used as the added alcohol to halt fermentation, imparting the sake with a rich and mushroomy flavour.

Lastly, one product that stood out as a distinctly regional creation was a Kokuto liqueur called 'Kokuto De Lequio.'

This liqueur was the brainchild of bartender Shingo Gokan, owner of the renowned cocktail bar El Lequio, a Latin and Ryukyu-inspired cocktail bar in Okinawa. The liqueur is a collaboration with Mizuho Shuzo, a local Gin and Awamori producer. Kokuto De Lequio is crafted using Awamori, Rum, and local Okinawan Kokuto sugar.

Below, you'll find a cocktail from El Lequio's Bar Manager, Satoshi Sugiura.

Kokuto de Tiramisu
Created by Satoshi Sugiura

45ml	Kokuto De Lequio
15ml	Mascarpone Cheese
55ml	Milk
10ml	Cold Brew Coffee

Glass:	Small Rocks
Method:	Shake & Strain
Ice:	Block Ice
Garnish:	Coco Powder

Comments:
This drink was on the Menu at El Lequio, Okinawa in September 2023.
I had the privilege of meeting Satoshi-san at El Lequio in 2023. As we were chatting, I asked about a the called 'Kokuto de Tiramisu.' Being a fan of anything with Kokuto sugar and a huge tiramisu enthusiast, I already knew I was going to love it. And indeed, I did, immensely, I even went back the next day to have it again.

Aromatised Shochu

Aromatised shochu is not technically a recognised category, and you won't encounter this term frequently. However, it broadly describes shochu varieties that incorporate ingredients other than the primary base ingredient we've already mentioned. As you already know, shochu production typically requires a fermentable sugar to create alcohol. Still, many approved ingredients lack sufficient fermentable sugars to produce a standalone product. While it is possible to create shochu exclusively from sources like milk or carrots, such examples are rare.

When using aromatising ingredients, the specifics of the production methods are normally unknown, but a simple rule is the aromatising ingredient is added during the second moromi to impart flavour. Examples of such ingredients include kelp, shiitake mushrooms, and matcha. As I write this, I have a bottle of green tea shochu across the room from me. The liquid is based on sweet potato, and during the second moromi, they incorporate Sencha tea for flavour.

One brand who has become quite successful with aromatised shochu is Beniotome shochu is located in Tanushimaru-machi, Kurume City, Fukuoka Prefecture. To my knowledge they are the only producer of Goma (sesame) shochu in Japan! The spring water from the Mino mountain range that rises behind the distillery is pure and very suitable for brewing. In the 1970s, when the popularity of western liquors increased, the founder of Beniotome, Haruno Hayashida, came up with shochu using sesame with the aim of "making a fragrant liquor that is as good as the western liquors that everyone admires."

(Side note, a favourite of mine is the Beniotome Kuro, which uses black koji).

The list of approved ingredients has expanded over time, and the National Tax Agency of Japan has shown no inclination to further expand it. Nevertheless, the current list is quite extensive, including some ingredients that are assumed to no longer be in production, like saffron.

Below, you'll find a compilation of cocktails made with aromatised Shochu. Given the uniqueness of each Shochu variety, I've chosen a few favourites from the submissions.

Phase Space
Created by Thomas Ryan-Tarrant

50ml	Beniotome Kuro Sesame Shochu
15ml	Matcha-Infused banana liqueur
10ml	Velvet Falernum
5ml	Cachaca
2 Dash	Ms Betters Mt Fuji Bitters

Glass:	Rocks
Method:	Stirred
Ice:	Block Ice
Garnish:	Banana chips dipped in chocolate

Comments:
This drink finds its inspiration in the concept of potential, particularly in the realm of quantum physics, where it mirrors the state preceding an event, such as a tasting, where all conceivable possibilities exist as truths. In other words, all the ingredients are flavours that can be skilfully adjusted or employed in diverse ways to cater to a broad spectrum of palates.

About this Shochu:
Benoitome Shuzo has crafted a uniquely refreshing and smokey Kuro sesame shochu. This exceptional spirit combines the rich, oak-barrel matured notes found in their finest shochu with the comforting warmth and umami depth of black sesame. Distinguished by a nuttier palate compared to traditional shochu, this black sesame shochu boasts a robust and invigorating aroma.

This shochu is brewed with black koji, known for its high citric acid content. This carefully crafted shochu develops its crisp, opulent flavours in the humid brewing conditions of the region. The resulting shochu has a fresh and pleasantly tart finish.

What Would Usagi-chan Drink?
Created by Caer Maiko Ferguson

45ml	Strawberry infused Rihei Ginger Shochu
20ml	Lemon Juice
20ml	Calpis Syrup
Top	Sparkling rosé

Glass:	Rocks
Method:	Stirred
Ice:	Block Ice
Garnish:	Banana chips dipped in chocolate

Comments:
This drink was take from the JSS Website.

Strawberry infused Rihei Ginger Shochu
150g	Strawberries
500ml	Rihei Ginger Shochu

Infuse for 6-24 hours in a cold space, until the shochu is red

Calpis Syrup
300ml	Calpis
300g	White Sugar

Mix together until sugar is dissolved.

About this Shochu:
This single-distilled, one of a kind shochu is made from ginger in Miyazaki prefecture. Rihei Ginger was born after local farmers came to the distillery requesting he craft a new shochu

made from their amazing quality ginger after Rihei had made a reputation for themselves using less common ingredients for their shochu.

Shochu Tasting Pages
Please uses these pages to document any shochu you've tried while reading this book.

Brand Name ....

Prefecture ....

Distillery/ Brewery ....

Rating ☆☆☆☆☆

Filtration ....

ABV ....

Yeast ....

GI ....

Koji
Rice - Barley - Sweet Potato

White - Black - Yellow
Other ....

Style
☐ Honkaku ☐ Konwa ☐ Korui

Shochu Type
☐ Imo
☐ Kome
☐ Kasutori
☐ Mugi
☐ Kokuto
☐ Soba
☐ Awamori
☐ Other ....

Other
☐ Genshu
☐ Kusu
☐ Other ....

Aging
Shitsugi   Cask

Other ....

Notes

_____

_____

_____

_____

_____

_____

Distillation Type

Vacuum   Atmospheric

Enjoyed
☐   Over Ice
☐   Oyuwari
☐   Mizuwari
☐   Sodawari
☐   Cocktail
☐   Chūhai
Other ....

Food Pairing

_____

Brand Name	....	**Style**
		☐ Honkaku ☐ Konwa ☐ Korui

Prefecture ....

Style
☐ Honkaku ☐ Konwa ☐ Korui

Shochu Type

Distillery/
Brewery ....
☐ Imo
☐ Kome
☐ Kasutori

Rating ☆☆☆☆☆
☐ Mugi
☐ Kokuto

Filtration ....
☐ Soba
☐ Awamori

ABV ....
☐ Other ....

Yeast ....

Other
☐ Genshu

GI ....
☐ Kusu
☐ Other ....

Koji
Rice - Barley - Sweet Potato

White - Black - Yellow
Other ....

Aging
Shitsugi   Cask

Other ....

Notes

_____

_____

_____

_____

_____

_____

Distillation Type

Vacuum   Atmospheric

Enjoyed
☐   Over Ice
☐   Oyuwari
☐   Mizuwari
☐   Sodawari
☐   Cocktail
☐   Chūhai
Other ....

Food Pairing

_____

Brand Name ....

Prefecture ....

Distillery/
Brewery ....

Rating ☆☆☆☆☆

Filtration ....

ABV ....

Yeast ....

GI ....

Koji
Rice - Barley - Sweet Potato

White - Black - Yellow
Other ....

Style
☐ Honkaku ☐ Konwa ☐ Korui

Shochu Type
☐ Imo
☐ Kome
☐ Kasutori
☐ Mugi
☐ Kokuto
☐ Soba
☐ Awamori
☐ Other ....

Other
☐ Genshu
☐ Kusu
☐ Other ....

Aging
Shitsugi   Cask

Other ....

Notes

_____

_____

_____

_____

_____

_____

Distillation Type

Vacuum   Atmospheric

Enjoyed
☐   Over Ice
☐   Oyuwari
☐   Mizuwari
☐   Sodawari
☐   Cocktail
☐   Chūhai
Other ....

Food Pairing

_____

| Brand Name | .... | **Style** |
| **Prefecture** | .... | ☐ Honkaku ☐ Konwa ☐ Korui |

Shochu Type

Distillery/
Brewery .... ☐ Imo
☐ Kome
Rating ☆☆☆☆☆ ☐ Kasutori
☐ Mugi
☐ Kokuto
Filtration .... ☐ Soba
☐ Awamori
ABV .... ☐ Other ....

Yeast .... **Other**
☐ Genshu
GI .... ☐ Kusu
☐ Other ....

Koji
Rice - Barley - Sweet Potato

Aging
White - Black - Yellow
Shitsugi   Cask
Other ....
Other ....

Notes

_____

_____

_____

_____

_____

_____

_____

Distillation Type

Vacuum   Atmospheric

Enjoyed
☐   Over Ice
☐   Oyuwari
☐   Mizuwari
☐   Sodawari
☐   Cocktail
☐   Chūhai
Other ....

Food Pairing

_____

Brand Name ....

Prefecture ....

Distillery/
Brewery ....

Rating ☆☆☆☆☆

Filtration ....

ABV ....

Yeast ....

GI ....

Koji
Rice - Barley - Sweet Potato

White - Black - Yellow
Other ....

Style
☐ Honkaku ☐ Konwa ☐ Korui

Shochu Type
☐ Imo
☐ Kome
☐ Kasutori
☐ Mugi
☐ Kokuto
☐ Soba
☐ Awamori
☐ Other ....

Other
☐ Genshu
☐ Kusu
☐ Other ....

Aging
Shitsugi   Cask

Other ....

Notes

_____

_____

_____

_____

_____

_____

Distillation Type

Vacuum   Atmospheric

Enjoyed
☐   Over Ice
☐   Oyuwari
☐   Mizuwari
☐   Sodawari
☐   Cocktail
☐   Chūhai
Other ....

Food Pairing

_____

Brand Name	....	Style
		☐ Honkaku ☐ Konwa ☐ Korui
Prefecture	....	

Shochu Type

Distillery/		☐ Imo
Brewery	....	☐ Kome
		☐ Kasutori
Rating	☆☆☆☆☆	☐ Mugi
		☐ Kokuto
Filtration	....	☐ Soba
		☐ Awamori
ABV	....	☐ Other ....
Yeast	....	**Other**
		☐ Genshu
GI	....	☐ Kusu
		☐ Other ....

Koji

Rice - Barley - Sweet Potato

White - Black - Yellow

Other ....

Aging

Shitsugi   Cask

Other ....

Notes

_____

_____

_____

_____

_____

_____

Distillation Type

Vacuum   Atmospheric

Enjoyed

☐	Over Ice
☐	Oyuwari
☐	Mizuwari
☐	Sodawari
☐	Cocktail
☐	Chūhai

Other ....

Food Pairing

_____

Brand Name	....	Style
		□ Honkaku □ Konwa □ Korui

Prefecture ....

Distillery/
Brewery ....

Rating ☆☆☆☆☆

Filtration ....

ABV ....

Yeast ....

GI ....

Koji
Rice - Barley - Sweet Potato

White - Black - Yellow
Other ....

Style
□ Honkaku □ Konwa □ Korui

Shochu Type
□ Imo
□ Kome
□ Kasutori
□ Mugi
□ Kokuto
□ Soba
□ Awamori
□ Other ....

Other
□ Genshu
□ Kusu
□ Other ....

Aging
Shitsugi   Cask

Other ....

Notes

_____

_____

_____

_____

_____

_____

Distillation Type

Vacuum   Atmospheric

Enjoyed
□ Over Ice
□ Oyuwari
□ Mizuwari
□ Sodawari
□ Cocktail
□ Chūhai
Other ....

Food Pairing

_____

Brand Name	....	**Style**

Brand Name ....

Prefecture ....

**Distillery/
Brewery** ....

Rating ☆☆☆☆☆

Filtration ....

ABV ....

Yeast ....

GI ....

Koji
Rice - Barley - Sweet Potato

White - Black - Yellow
Other ....

Style
☐ Honkaku ☐ Konwa ☐ Korui

Shochu Type
☐ Imo
☐ Kome
☐ Kasutori
☐ Mugi
☐ Kokuto
☐ Soba
☐ Awamori
☐ Other ....

Other
☐ Genshu
☐ Kusu
☐ Other ....

Aging
Shitsugi   Cask

Other ....

Notes
_____
_____
_____
_____
_____
_____

Distillation Type

Vacuum   Atmospheric

Enjoyed
☐ Over Ice
☐ Oyuwari
☐ Mizuwari
☐ Sodawari
☐ Cocktail
☐ Chūhai
Other ....

Food Pairing
_____

Brand Name ....

Prefecture ....

Distillery/
Brewery ....

Rating ☆☆☆☆☆

Filtration ....

ABV ....

Yeast ....

GI ....

Koji
Rice - Barley - Sweet Potato

White - Black - Yellow
Other ....

Style
☐ Honkaku ☐ Konwa ☐ Korui

Shochu Type
☐ Imo
☐ Kome
☐ Kasutori
☐ Mugi
☐ Kokuto
☐ Soba
☐ Awamori
☐ Other ....

Other
☐ Genshu
☐ Kusu
☐ Other ....

Aging
Shitsugi   Cask

Other ....

Notes

_____

_____

_____

_____

_____

_____

_____

Distillation Type

Vacuum   Atmospheric

Enjoyed
☐   Over Ice
☐   Oyuwari
☐   Mizuwari
☐   Sodawari
☐   Cocktail
☐   Chūhai
Other ....

Food Pairing

_____

Brand Name	....	**Style**		

Brand Name ....

Prefecture ....

Distillery/ Brewery ....

Rating ☆☆☆☆☆

Filtration ....

ABV ....

Yeast ....

GI ....

Koji
Rice - Barley - Sweet Potato

White - Black - Yellow
Other ....

Style
☐ Honkaku ☐ Konwa ☐ Korui

Shochu Type
☐ Imo
☐ Kome
☐ Kasutori
☐ Mugi
☐ Kokuto
☐ Soba
☐ Awamori
☐ Other ....

Other
☐ Genshu
☐ Kusu
☐ Other ....

Aging
Shitsugi   Cask

Other ....

Notes

_____

_____

_____

_____

_____

_____

Distillation Type

Vacuum   Atmospheric

Enjoyed
☐   Over Ice
☐   Oyuwari
☐   Mizuwari
☐   Sodawari
☐   Cocktail
☐   Chūhai
Other ....

Food Pairing

_____

CHAPTER SIX
CHUHAI

Chuhai, short for "shōchū highball," is a common "cocktail" frequently enjoyed by many young Japanese nationals. Unlike the world-famous whisky highball, chuhai is shochu-based and should not be confused with it.

In the UK, any alcoholic beverage with three or more ingredients is classified as a cocktail. So technically, we would consider these drinks as cocktails. However, in Japan, they are simply known as Chuhai and not viewed as cocktails.

While whisky highballs are made with blended Scotch whisky and soda, chuhai is typically based on Korui shōchū and carbonated water, flavoured with lemon, grapefruit, or other fruits. Chuhai usually offers a wider range of flavours compared to Highballs.

Chuhai are available in cans as ready-to-drink (RTD) beverages, with an alcohol content ranging from 3% to 9%. However, discerning Izakaya can be seen making Chuhai with Honkaku shochu and other unique flavours. What distinguishes them from mass-produced counterparts is the meticulous attention to detail, the use of premium ingredients, and the artisanal approach to crafting each drink.

Authors thoughts
I have a deep affection for Chuhai. To me, they encapsulate what I cherish in mixology. While intricate cocktails with all their technological wizardry can be entertaining, I have a

special fondness for the straightforwardness of a single flavour taking the spotlight in a drink (one of my all time favourite drink is Apples from Coupette in London). When you indulge in Chuhai, you're not searching for a mixological masterpiece; they're enjoyable, uncomplicated, and simply delicious. I look forward to a time when bartenders embrace Chuhai and transform them in the same way they've innovated with Highballs.

Yuzu Chuhai
Created by Samuel Boulton

25ml	Okinawa gin
25ml	Tatenokawa Kodakara Yuzu shochu liquor
Top	Soda or Lemonade

Glass:	Highball with cubed ice
Method:	Build
Garnish:	Lemon Peel

Plum Chuhai
Created by Samuel Boulton

25ml	Aged Mugi shochu
25ml	Tatenokawa Kodakara Umeshu
Top	Ginger ale

Glass:	Highball with cubed ice
Method:	Build
Garnish:	Orange Peel

Lychee Chuhai

Created by Samuel Boulton

25ml	Kokuto shochu
25ml	Gabriel Boudier Lychee liquor
Top	Lemonade

Glass:	Highball with cubed ice
Method:	Build
Garnish:	Lemon Penny

Mango & Ginger Chuhai
Created by Samuel Boulton

25ml	Soba shochu
25ml	Tatenokawa Kodakara Mango shochu liquor
Top	Ginger ale

Glass:	Highball with cubed ice
Method:	Build
Garnish:	Lemon Peel

Flora Chuhai
Created by Samuel Boulton

25ml	Kasutori shochu
25ml	Muyu Jasmine
Top	Tonic

Glass:	Highball with cubed ice
Method:	Build
Garnish:	Lemon Peel

CHAPTER SEVEN
KOJI WHISKEY

Commodore Matthew Perry, who arrived in Tokyo Bay, wielding the might of gunboat diplomacy. Perry's mission was to secure Japan as a refuelling station for coal-powered vessels, quell hostilities against foreigners, and initiate trade with global powers. As part of his diplomatic efforts, Perry brought with him a variety of gifts, including barrels of whiskey, marking the inception of whiskey's introduction to Japan.

Several months later, in the Kaga Domain, now part of Toyama Prefecture, a brilliant mind was born on November 3, 1854: Jokichi Takamine. The son of a Samurai Physician and his mother from a sake-making family, young Takamine displayed exceptional intelligence. His journey of learning took him to Nagasaki, where he studied "Dutch Learning," acquiring knowledge of speaking in Dutch and English, and the learning of the wider world. At the age of 13, he began military training and high school, eventually graduating from Tokyo University's School of Engineering as the top student. In his early twenties, Takamine ventured abroad to Glasgow University, where he studied Western industrial practices, foreshadowing a similar path taken by Masataka Taketsuru.

Returning to Japan, Takamine assumed a role in the Department of Agriculture and Commerce in Tokyo, tasked with modernising key Japanese industries. One of his exciting challenges was to revolutionise sake brewing, no doubt where he learned in-depth about Koji. In 1884, he embarked on a life-changing journey to the World's Exposition in New Orleans, marking his first visit to the United States.

In New Orleans, Takamine found more than just inspiration; he fell in love with Caroline "Carrie" Hitch. Determined to marry her, he returned to Japan to amass the wealth necessary for their union. He briefly served as the interim director of Japan's patent office and later founded Asia's first superphosphate (chemical fertiliser) mine, which quickly enriched him. In 1887, he returned to New Orleans and married Caroline.

Although Caroline relocated to Tokyo with her husband, she found the cultural differences and anti-foreigner movement of the time to be overwhelming.

Nevertheless, she gave birth to two children during their stay in Tokyo, Jokichi, Jr. and Ebenezer. Three years later, in 1890, a business offer from Caroline's mother, the family returned to the United States, where they founded the Takamine Ferment Company.

By 1891, he had patented the Takamine Process. A method of using koji for scarification in alcohol production, instead of malting, in both the US and the UK. In that same year, Caroline's mother introduced him to Joseph Greenhut, the president of the Illinois Whisky Trust (the largest producer of distilled spirits in America during the late 19th century), to which Takamine licensed them a patent for the use of the Takamine Process (licensing a patent was not a common Japanese business practise and shows the forward thinking Takamine had).

In 1891 they began experiments to make Koji Whiskey at their Manhattan Distillery in Peoria, IL. The production of kome koji whisky was revolutionary, promoting fermentation at a lower cost and within a shorter period of time compared to conventional whisky production with barley malt, cutting out the malt process altogether (this didn't please the local malting industry).

The Takamine Process had the potential to fundamentally change the landscape of whiskey production. Despite initial setbacks, experiments resumed, leading to commercial production approval in December 1894.

Unfortunately, in February 1895, the State of Illinois and the Justice Department enforced the Sherman Act (an anti trust act), which dismantled the Illinois Whisky Trust. As a consequence, the Manhattan Distillery was sold to new owners and was then reverted to malting, at this time, Takamine also lost his patent in a legal battle.

To help understand the time line this was 1895 and Takamine was in America trying to make "Japanese whiskey" the very same year Masataka Taketsuru, the father of Japanese whisky we know today was born.

While the Koji whisky was being developing, Takamine established the Takamine International Ferment Company, isolating Taka Diastase, a koji-based digestive aid, and licensing it to Park Davis Company (now Pfizer). He also set up an import company in Japan to import Taka Diastase, (which later become Daiichi Sankyo which is still in business today).

At the age of 40, in his Harlem laboratory, Takamine achieved a groundbreaking milestone by isolating adrenaline, the first human hormone ever isolated. This discovery's impact is still felt today, as adrenaline continues to save lives in hospitals worldwide.

Takamine's influence extended to both Japan and the United States. He received a gift of the Japan Pavilion structure from the Emperor of Japan after the St. Louis World's Fair, which now stands as Shofuden in the Catskills. In 1905, he established the Nippon Club, a private gentlemen's club in New York City, catering to Japanese businessmen, and donated cherry trees to Washington, D.C., although he insisted on attributing the gesture to Tokyo's Mayor, Yukio Ozaki.

Jokichi Takamine passed away at the age of 67 on July 22, 1922, and is interred at Woodlawn Cemetery in the Bronx. His legacy endures through Takamine Whiskey, produced at the Shinozaki Distillery in Fukuoka, Japan, honouring his pioneering spirit and enduring contributions.

Modern Day Takamine

Takamine 8-Year Whiskey, is from Shinozaki Distillery nestled in the heart of Asakura, Fukuoka, established in 1922.

At the heart of Takamine Whiskey lies the innovative Takamine Process, a patented technique that pays homage to tradition while laying new ground for whisky production. Unlike conventional malt whisky production, this Takamine Process sees both koji and yeast working in a 15-day multiple parallel fermentation, using Kyokai #2 Yeast and White Koji, resulting in a unique profile for Takamine whiskies.

After the multiple parallel fermentation, the 100% barley mash is double pot-distilled. Takamine 8-year then patiently rests in a blend of 90% virgin American oak and 10% ex-Bourbon casks.

Modern Day Koji Whisky

On February 12, 2021, the Japan Spirits & Liqueurs Makers Association (JSLMA) unveiled their official Labelling Standards with the goal of defining what qualifies as "Japanese whisky." This announcement was met with widespread international acclaim. After years of uncertainty where spirits labeled as Japanese whisky might have been Scotch (or other whiskey) imported and only bottled in Japan, these guidelines marked a significant stride towards transparency in the industry. However, within these regulations, a notable omission is the treatment of koji whisky.

The traditional koji fermentation process has been integral to food and alcohol production in Japan for countless centuries. Surprisingly, JSLMA's new guidelines completely overlook the role of koji in whisky production and explicitly forbid its use in conjunction with the designation of "Japanese whisky." One of the guidelines stipulates the use of malted grains, a standard saccharification practice found in Scotch, Irish, and other whisky styles.

Koji Whiskey Cocktail
Shift Drink
Created by Jane Nam

45ml	Takamine 8 year
22.5ml	Colorful Sweet Potato Shochu
22.5ml	Coconut water
22.5ml	Osmanthus Peach tea syrup
2 Dash	Angostura bitters

Glass:	Nick & Nora or Teacup
Method:	Stirred
Ice:	None
Garnish:	Fresh Osmanthus flowers or a candied peach

Comments:
Build in a mixing vessel, give it a short stir, just until lightly chilled. You don't need too much dilution because of the coconut water.

Jane works at a lovely little bar, at the end of the evening Jane takes away all the menus and ask everyone in the room if they would like to share a shift drink with her. Jane says "This small ritual is a way to bring the customers a bit closer to me, to share my sense of self and taste, as well as an offer of something they probably would not order on their own. Takamine is one of the more interesting whiskies I've tried. It starts off with a sharp, earthy walnut note, which I tempered with the softness of coconut water. But there are also notes of stone fruits, and those I brought out with a floral peach tea syrup. The colorful shochu gives it added complexity and helps the cocktail finish off with a bit of biscuity sweetness."

CHAPTER EIGHT
KOJI VODKA

Koji might not be the first thing you consider when looking to produce vodka. As vodka is typically highly rectified, this results in a reduction in the umami impact that koji will have. However, the resulting vodkas can be exquisite. One example is Haku Vodka, made by the renowned spirits company Suntory.

Founded in 1899, the House of Suntory was built on Shinjiro Torii's dream of creating exceptional Japanese spirits using the country's natural resources and craftsmanship. Overcoming challenges, Suntory produced wine, whisky, brandy, and introduced Hermes Vodka in 1956.

Haku means "white" in Japanese and can also be interpreted as "brilliant," which they say is "a reflection of the craftsmanship of creating a clear and clean-tasting vodka." Made from 100% Japanese white rice, double distilled, and filtered through bamboo charcoal, Haku Vodka has a uniquely soft, round, and subtly sweet flavour.

Haku is a testament to Suntory's craftsmanship, starting with Japanese rice fermented with rice koji to create a mash. The first distillation takes place in Kagoshima using traditional stainless steel reduced-pressure pot stills, resulting in a shochu-style spirit. This spirit is then divided into two batches. One batch undergoes a traditional vodka column still distillation at their Osaka distillery, producing a clean and delicate vodka. The other batch is distilled at their Chita distillery using a lower-reflux column setup, resulting in a richer vodka with a stronger rice flavour compared to the Osaka still. These two batches are blended to achieve a harmonious balance of flavours and texture, ensuring complexity and smoothness. Finally, the vodka is filtered through bamboo charcoal to create the finished product.

Haku Vodka offers a complex profile with notes of cardamom, bitter lemon, mint leaves, mango sticky rice, resinous tree sap, and a lingering sweet peppermint finish.

Koji Martini
Created by James Bowker

60ml	Haku
10ml	Junmai Sake
5ml	Dry Vermouth
4 Drops	Aged Mirin

Glass:	Martini
Method:	Stirred
Ice:	None
Garnish:	Lemon twist (discarded)

CHAPTER NINE
FINAL THOUGHTS

As we come to the end of our journey through the enchanting world of Koji, sake, shochu and cocktails, it's time to reflect on the significance of Koji, which has only recently reached the western palate. Koji, with its millennia-old history, is a testament to the enduring traditions of asian cuisine. Its introduction to the western culinary scene is like discovering a hidden treasure, one that has the potential to bring a new world into the art of mixology.

I sincerely hope that the Koji revolution we've explored in this book continues to flourish. The Koji culture, so deeply intertwined with Japanese culinary heritage, has already made its mark within categories I love like sake and shochu. As these categories gain recognition and appreciation beyond Japan, they open up exciting possibilities for creative mixologists, chefs, and home enthusiasts worldwide.

"The Art of Mixing Koji Cocktails" is but a glimpse into the vast universe of possibilities that Koji offers. It serves as an introduction to the myriad flavours that can be unlocked through this miraculous mould. As you embark on your own Koji cocktail adventures, remember that this book is merely the beginning of what the world of Koji has to offer.

With every cocktail you craft and every sip you savour, you become a part of the growing Koji movement, a movement that celebrates tradition, innovation, and the timeless art of transforming humble ingredients into exquisite drinks. So, raise your glass to the past, present, and future of Koji, and may your mixing journey be as rich and diverse as the history of this remarkable microorganism. Here is to the endless possibilities that lie ahead

Kanpai!

ABOUT THE AUTHOR

My journey into the world of bartending started midway through university when I realised that performing arts wasn't the right career path for me. While pursuing my studies, I found myself bartending on the side, like many students do, and it seemed to be a reasonable fit. So, I stuck with it. Several years later, I've now been a bartender for over a decade, and I've mostly taught myself the craft through extensive reading, attending talks, and of course, a lot of trial and error.

My fascination with sake began in 2017 while planning a trip to Japan with an ex-girlfriend who, to my chagrin at the time, wasn't keen on planning. I spent six months diving deep into Japanese culture and discovered sake along the way. As part of our trip, we visited the Akashi-Tai Sake Brewery in Hyogo Prefecture, which opened my eyes to the vast world of sake. This newfound interest prompted me to dedicate more time to learning about sake and sharing my knowledge with friends and patrons.

In 2018, I took a significant step by opening my first bar, The Vanguard, located in Birmingham's historic Jewellery Quarter. It was the UK's first Cocktails Bar & Meadery. After establishing a name for myself in the mead industry and launching my first brand, The Modern Mead Co, my team and I outgrew The Vanguard, leading us to set our sights on a larger project.

In September 2020, amid a global pandemic, I proudly launched The Pineapple Club in Birmingham's Great Western Arcade. The Pineapple Club garnered a slew of awards upon its opening, including recognition from the CLASS Awards 2022, where we won Bar Employer of the Year, and The Drinks Trust Golden Pineapple 2022 for Best Internal Staff Initiatives. In 2022, we also received accolades from the 2022 Spirited Awards, ranking as a Regional Top 10 Honouree for Best New International Bar in Europe. Furthermore, we secured the 14th spot on the UK's Top 50 Cocktail Bars list for 2023.

In September 2021, I reached another significant milestone by publishing my debut book, titled "The Vermouth Ambassador's Guide to Modern Drinking." Vermouth held a special place in my heart as it was my initial passion. I aspired to establish a career in the world of Vermouth. However, I soon realised that my heritage, which didn't align with the traditional Vermouth producing regions like Italy, Spain, or France, presented challenges in pursuing the roles I aspired to. This made the industry appear rather unwelcoming to outsiders like me.

In October 2022, I unveiled Shibuya Underground, a basement level omakase-style sake and cocktail bar featuring two distinct menus: one offering six courses of Japanese-inspired cocktails and the other presenting a six-course sake experience. As part of my commitment to formalise my expertise, I embarked on a journey to enhance my knowledge. It began with my pursuit of the WSET Level 3 in Sake, which, to my initial dismay, resulted in failure. However, this setback only fuelled my determination. I despised the idea of failure and delved into an intensive study of sake and shochu, completing various courses, including John Gauntner's Certified Sake Professional, Japanese Sake Academy's Sake Expert, Michael Tremblay's Sake Scholar Course 2023, and the ISS Shochu Advisor programme.

In 2022, I was honoured to be invited by the International Wine and Spirits Challenge to serve as a judge for the Shochu and sake categories, alongside other industry experts.

This book is the culmination of my journey of learning and discovery. My goal is to share my passion with fellow bartenders and demonstrate how these remarkable products can be integrated into western cocktails, enriching our menus and social gatherings. My journey in the world of sake and shochu continues, and I'm excited to see where it will lead me next.